THE END GAME

Kira —
Hope You Enjoy!
Warm Regards
Melissa

THE END GAME

The Laboratory Owner's Exit Strategy

Melissa Butterworth
CEO, Advanced Strategic Partners

Paperback ISBN: 978-1-7329555-0-9

Hardcover ISBN: 978-1-7329555-3-0

Ebook ISBN: 978-1-7329555-1-6

Library of Congress Control Number: 2019900766

Library of Congress Cataloging-in-Publication Data on file with the Publisher

Advanced Strategic Partners

www.AdvancedStrategicPartners.com

M18butterworth@advancedstrategicpartners.com

10 9 8 7 6 5 4 3 2

Printed in the USA.

Production & Design by Concierge Marketing, Inc.
www.ConciergeMarketing.com

Dedication

I dedicate this book to "P Daddy." You know who you are. You have been an angel sent from God throughout my career, and I am forever grateful for the impact that you have had on so many lives, including mine. You took the road less traveled and never gave up on your dream of reaching the top. You achieved it in a way that validated to me that there is a very humorous God.

Also, you showed up in my life when I had hit bottom, giving me a few breaks along the way when I needed them the most, reminding me again that there is a giving and humorous God. May God continue shining His blessings on you and your family for all of the hardship that you have endured to climb your way to the top. You always chose to take the high road and, unlike many others, helped so many people along the way. You are a man of honor, and I appreciate everything you stand for and, again, your continued belief in me.

I also dedicate this book to the laboratory business owners and executives who hired our firm along the way and to those of you who are currently thinking about selling or buying a company.

It has and will continue to be our team's great pleasure to make you more knowledgeable and informed so that you can successfully exit your business while maintaining as much of its original vision and integrity while maximizing your profits.

Contents

Introduction

The primary purpose of this book is to present precisely how to maximize the value of your laboratory business to gain the most financial return at the final sale.

Before I get into the details about the laboratory transaction process, it should be stated that having an industry-specific laboratory expert on your team when taking your company to the market is essential if you wish to maximize its value. You need an expert who has worked with multiple sellers and, more important, qualified buyers in the laboratory industry. This is one of the first steps you should take if you wish to receive the maximum value of what is likely the most important asset you own. This statement cannot be stressed enough.

If you only get one message from this book, this is the most significant. Once again: Hire an industry-specific laboratory expert to represent you and your laboratory when you decide it's time to sell your business. There is no substitute for his or her relationships and experience. No matter how sharp or educated you may be, a lack of experience in understanding how each potential buyer is measuring your company's metrics can and will translate into reduced dollars for the sale of your business. The right specialist will pay for himself or herself in a successful transaction.

Just because you know—or think you know—your business, that doesn't mean that you are mentally prepared to handle the institutional or strategic buyer who is assessing the potential value. They will be using their own specific metrics to reach their conclusions about the value of your business. In addition, the right intermediary will understand all the key negotiation and operational points as you construct the transition services agreement, which will have the biggest impact on your community, employees, patients, and customers.

Although companies change hands every day, selling and buying businesses can mean many things and take many forms.

- Who or what is being sold?
- How do you value the business and determine the sale price?
- Who is the best buyer for your company?
- What kind of transaction is it, and what are the tax consequences to the buyer and the seller?
- How long will the transaction take, and what is needed in due diligence?

These are only a few of the considerations in any given merger or acquisition. The process can become extremely confusing and overwhelming.

As a result, business owners can get exasperated when it comes time to sell their business or acquire a new company. This is the primary reason I decided to write this book.

As I was completing this book, we closed on a deal where we were able to secure our seller an additional $10+ million for his business from the same buyer who had made him an initial offer five months prior to his hiring our firm. How is that possible? Again, we can't stress enough the importance of hiring a team of knowledgeable, industry-specific experts to assist you in your laboratory transaction.

The second purpose of this book is to educate you on the six key steps of the merger and acquisition process and specific action items that you should implement during this process. We will take you through the process that my firm, Advanced Strategic Partners, has taken dozens of clients through over the last decade. This information has been compiled from multiple sources and, more important, from having personally and professionally taken the road less traveled in my career.

I have condensed years of firsthand laboratory industry expertise into this book. My team has spoken at seminars, made hundreds of presentations, toured, and met with dozens of laboratory owners throughout the United States. We have offered advice and information on the topics covered in this book. This book is intended to be a comprehensive guide to what can be a challenging process.

I guarantee that you will complete this book feeling more educated, confident, and knowledgeable about how the lab transaction process works, making you ready to embark on this next step of your life.

About Deal Extracts

Many chapters include actual stories about laboratory buyers and sellers that we have encountered throughout the years. The names of these sellers and buyers will remain anonymous for confidentiality reasons. They will be identified as "deal extracts." Some of these deals closed and some did not. These are stories of inspiration, integrity, greed, and, in some cases, outright stupidity. Some are useful and educational, and some are just plain entertaining. In deal making, as with other parts of life, reality is often stranger than fiction.

I have assembled some files and documents that go along with this book. They will be made available to potential sellers and buyers who schedule a face-to-face meeting and sign an exclusive representation agreement with my firm during the decision-making process of identifying your professional team of advisors. This highly sought-after confidential data package includes the following:

- Sample of a laboratory stock purchase agreement (SPA) and a laboratory asset purchase agreement (APA).

- A more detailed list of information that will be requested of the seller upon entering into the due diligence process with a buyer. Because the due diligence request list included in this book is fairly brief, this list has been assembled from various buyers and sellers throughout the years and is thorough, though by no means a "one size fits all."

- Two deal modeling spreadsheets used by buyers. One is from a large strategic buyer, and one is from a financial private equity group. We suspect that you will find it interesting to see how buyers view an acquisition.

- A transition services agreement (TSA).

- A standard confidentiality agreement (CA).

- A standard noncompete agreement (NC).

- A standard nondisclosure agreement (NDA).

- A standard letter of intent (LOI).

This package can be obtained by emailing and scheduling a face-to-face meeting with me. I look forward to hearing from you when you are ready to take this step.

m18butterworth@advancedstrategicpartners.com

1

My Life as an M&A Advisor and Deal Maker

I love my profession and am blessed to do what I do. I didn't get here by chance, and I know that I am fulfilling my life's ultimate purpose. I knew that I was meant to be in sales since the age of six, when I was constantly looking for ways to make money by serving others. I started by selling lemonade, cookies, and brownies as an entrepreneur with my own corner street stand in the neighborhood where I grew up in Harrisonburg, Virginia.

By the time I was in high school, I was selling tennis rackets and designer sports clothing. I spent one summer when I was sixteen doing community service at the local blood bank where I was fascinated by helping people and learned about the medical world and laboratory environment through this experience.

I graduated from college at the University of North Florida with dual degrees in marketing and management. I took advantage of the university's career development center, including resume development, interview preparation, and interviews with companies that were seeking recent graduates. I interviewed with as many companies as possible to gain the experience. I wanted a job in medical sales. After receiving three job offers from various nonmedical companies, I turned them all down. My father wasn't happy with me and thought that I should take the job with Enterprise Rent-A-Car for $28,000 a year.

I was more determined than ever to land a job in the medical industry and would spend the next five months broke and coming up with creative ways to land my medical sales dream job.

The local news station had interviewed me several months prior about my thoughts on the job market, as a recent college graduate. I took clips of that interview segment and created a two-minute video introducing myself to prospective medical companies. In this video, I focused on what I would contribute to the companies' bottom line by hiring me as a sales representative.

I researched the top fifty pharmaceutical companies and sent the resume video to the VP of human resources and sales VPs of all fifty of these companies. Sixty days later, I landed my first job out of college working as a pharmaceutical sales representative marketing two products: one for burn victims and the other for patients suffering from travelers' diarrhea. These products weren't the most glamorous products to be selling, but I knew that I was meant to help people, and I instantly felt that I was making a difference. I didn't reach my goal of making six figures my first year out of college, but I was much closer than I would have been had I settled for one of those other job offers.

After a year of selling pharmaceuticals to physicians who could rarely afford me five minutes of their time during an already crazy schedule, I made the decision to go into laboratory diagnostic sales. This was one of the best career decisions that I ever made. It was the mid-1990s, and the blood business was booming.

I spent the next nine years helping a group of pathologists grow an amazing laboratory from its early inception to over $45 million in annual sales. It was the best education ever. I learned how to draw blood, spin down specimens, courier blood work, put together marketing materials, sell, hire sales and service representatives, negotiate managed care contracts, open and build out patient service centers, and compete against the largest laboratories in the world. I loved taking the road less traveled and enjoyed using my creative side to successfully compete against the larger laboratories.

Having grown up as a competitive tennis player, winning was the only terminology in my vocabulary. One of the greatest career lessons that I learned watching my mother's career with Dell was to ensure that I negotiated equity ownership in any future company that I joined. I spent my twenties working eighteen-hour days building a company that made others millions. I wouldn't make that mistake again.

By the time I was thirty-four, I was making multiple six figures in the laboratory industry. I had managed to climb the corporate ladder through good old-fashioned hard work. I joined a company based out of Canada as the VP of managed care and was the regional VP of sales for the Southeast division. Dynacare Laboratory went public in the US in the late 1990s. They rewarded my stellar sales performance with stock options. I was at the top of my game in a thriving industry.

It wasn't unusual for top salespeople to make as much money or more than the physicians we serviced. The average total income easily surpassed $350,000 for a salesperson. The exceptional sales executives were surpassing $500,000 a year. Once Dynacare sold to one of the largest laboratories in the world, most of my counterparts started their own competitive laboratories. Ironically, my company ended up being the broker to sell some of their laboratories years later.

Their bold risk-taking paid off, and I often daydreamed about what my life would have looked like had I joined them instead of allowing my career to temporarily derail into corporate America. I witnessed many of them cash out and make between $20 million and $60 million. The big lesson I learned from this experience was that hard work combined with risk equals great reward. I am proud of those few who took this path. They truly took the road less traveled.

When Dynacare was sold, I made the decision to stay for the five-year period that my stock options would take to fully vest. I had an amazing four-year-and-331-day journey as the number one sales producer for that company, running their hospital division in the Southeast. I was making incredible money and enjoyed building a successful sales team that would continue ranking as the number one sales team year after year.

During the third year with that company, one of my favorite people (a boss and mentor) passed away. They replaced him with someone whom I considered to be your typical corporate yes man. Even though I was the number one producer in the entire country for four consecutive years, I was eventually fired. It made complete sense when I look back at the situation. I don't say that with any hesitation or sarcasm, as I now understand that corporate America isn't necessarily for everyone.

Initially, I was devastated because I loved my career and was exceptional at what I did. I had no idea where I would go to make the kind of money that I was accustomed to. Little did I know that God had a much greater plan for my future.

I formed my own company, Advanced Strategic Partners, in 2007—three months after I lost my job. It was created through a vision that I had while living in my apartment in South Florida. I drove throughout the southeastern US and talked with as many lab owners as I could. I wanted to better understand their challenges and what they thought about selling their laboratories. The timing was perfect, and the market was about to boom as the consolidation of the laboratory industry started to escalate.

I was at the right place at the perfect time—born to do this for a living. My friends often say that if they had to go to war with one person, they would choose me. I won't take no for an answer, and I follow through on everything. I am extremely competitive, persistent, positive, fearless, determined, honest, and loyal. These are the attributes that have allowed me to excel at my chosen profession. If I am hired to represent you and your company, I will exceed your expectations.

Looking back, I understand that I was never meant to work inside the limitations presented in corporate America. I enjoy representing the small to midsized laboratories who have chosen to take the road less traveled and to fearlessly compete against the larger labs. Remember, this was the path that I had been on from the inception of my career. I was now back on the path where I belonged, so being fired was clearly a blessing. I was now in a position to help laboratory owners achieve financial freedom and recognize their own "end game," hence, the name of my book.

There does come a point when most business owners need to make the important decision to climb to the next level. This is where our team at Advanced Strategic Partners comes into play. We have all been on both sides of the mergers and acquisition or M&A process. All of the executives on our team have worked for various laboratories throughout their careers. We are 100 percent focused on laboratory M&A work and will give you our undivided attention throughout the entire M&A process.

Many of my colleagues have asked me what an M&A advisor is and how they can become one. I've included some stories for you to read. They aren't so much about the art of the deal, but rather about what being an M&A advisor entails.

How We Get Our New Clients

All of our business is word of mouth through our contacts and industry relationships. We don't take on every business that contacts us and purposely choose our clients wisely. We are proud of this because we have worked hard to achieve this status. For example, we no longer spend countless hours convincing anyone to sell. We view our role as an advisor who provides data based on facts occurring at any given point in time. We will make recommendations, and it's ultimately up to our clients to make the best informed decisions.

We receive a lot of calls and emails, with the biggest question being, "What is my business worth?" We prefer not to give an answer until we know more about the business. We don't want to set expectations too high, because it is exceedingly harder to lower them later.

Once we gain a better understanding of our potential client's business, including the financials, contracts, geographical coverage, volumes, and types of tests, we provide them with a ballpark estimate.

Meeting with New Laboratory Owners

Other than the days when we close business deals, the best part of our job is going out to meet with business owners and discovering the inner workings of the laboratory. During these visits we learn about the company history, where the business is now, and, most important for selling a business, what the financials and potential growth opportunities are.

During this initial meeting, we review our process and determine if there is a good fit between the seller and our team. Once this is established, we determine what the next steps are and how to best proceed.

Negotiations

There are many times when weekends and late nights are common for M&A advisors. I remember doing final negotiations while in the airport coming back from a family wedding one Sunday afternoon.

We were down to two buyers who had proposed similar offers. Both were nearing the limit of how much they were willing to offer. It all came down to how quickly the buyers were willing to close the deal. It was tough on the seller because he liked both buyers. One buyer was willing to close in less than sixty days, and our seller made the decision to move forward with the more aggressive buyer. He was concerned that a longer closing period could cause potential disruptions to his business.

We finalized the letter of intent with the buyer the next morning, and a deal was struck. We entered a thirty-day due diligence period and closed within two months.

Greed

There is often a lot of money up for grabs in an M&A transaction. I find it interesting to witness the struggle with greed that many endure as a deal progresses. Some sellers swear allegiance to their employees and speak of the bonuses these employees will receive. As the closing nears, that talk gets quieter and eventually fades away. Others talk little but end up delivering to key employees.

Some inherently know what their responsibilities are after the sale. Unfortunately, you can't completely walk away after selling a business. There are tax, environmental, and other liabilities that remain with a seller for a while. Others try to slide as much of the responsibility to the other side of the table. Although that may not be viewed as honorable, it is ethical as long as the conversation is open and transparent. Several business owners I have dealt with have gone too far by not disclosing potential liabilities, which can cause problems and ill will.

The worst time to try to settle company ownership issues is when there is an offer on the table and money is up for grabs. Given a choice between being fair and reasonable and walking away with $100,000, many will choose the money. This is why, when our firm signs an engagement letter, we explore the ownership structure and try to ferret out any potential problems. If there are issues, we will recommend that sellers get an attorney involved and properly document the ownership of the business.

After years of experiencing these types of situations, I'm rarely surprised at how some people behave when there is a large amount of money involved. The worst behavior we have witnessed was with a client who talked a lot about integrity and honesty, but after the sale, we learned that six months prior to selling, he had bought out his partner for $250,000. He told him that the company was going bankrupt and that he was about to close the doors, offering him $250,000 for his ownership in the company.

Of course, the partner took the money, only to learn that the company was sold six months later for $41 million. The ex-partner was so infuriated that he assaulted the seller in his own front yard after learning about the sale.

We also represented a client for the better part of a year on the seller's side. They were a family-owned laboratory with a cast of characters unlike any other we have ever met. After we spent a year introducing them to our industry contacts, they made the decision not to sell. Almost sixteen months later, one of the buyers whom we introduced them to ended up purchasing the company. One of the main owners had suddenly passed away, and they were ready to sell. We had contacted them to discuss representing them again, considering we had already prepared them for the sale and had introduced them to all of our contacts. They made the decision to represent themselves and work directly with the buyers. This was the only time that this had ever happened to our firm.

The irony behind it was that the buyer had hired our firm to assist in several transactions that were occurring that same year. They had told us that they were aware of all the work we had done representing this seller and would be happy to pay us our fee since it was ethically the right thing to do. We appreciated their loyalty to us and asked them to simply continue using our services down the road.

The key executive of this buyer is now one of the highest-ranking executives for one of the largest laboratories in the world and recently completed another deal with our firm. The laboratory that had decided not to use our services left over $12 million on the table because they didn't know the financial metrics that the buyer was using. The $12 million would have been after they paid our fee.

What is the best part of being an M&A advisor? The closing!

Deal Extract

We once sold a private laboratory that had various service lines. For example, they sold lab services to physician offices, corporate accounts, nursing homes, assisted living facilities, and patients who needed home care services.

There are always challenges in selling any business. For this one, it was the fact that the buyer wanted to offload a portion of the soon-to-be acquired business by potentially simultaneously closing with a third party.

The buyer did not disclose these facts with our firm until after our client had accepted their letter of intent (LOI). This was a complete surprise and something that we were less than thrilled about. We had been promised a thirty-day due diligence time frame. This would never happen if we allowed a third party into our due diligence. It had the capability of backfiring and wrecking the entire deal, and we knew it.

We felt that we were backed against the wall when we were communicated this additional information so late in the game. Ultimately, our client made the decision to allow the buyer to bring in the third party. The thirty-day due diligence turned into sixty and started heading toward ninety. As suspected, the third party was much slower at cyphering through the due diligence than our seller and the primary buyer.

It was a long and tough few months for our team. Our seller finally made the decision to take one of the business segments off the table and sell a portion of his business. In retrospect, it was the right decision. When you start adding third parties into the mix and trying to accomplish a simultaneous closing, things can derail quickly.

It is tempting to celebrate the sale of a business once you get the LOI and start circulating the purchase agreement. However, we have learned to wait a bit. In fact, sometimes I hold my breath, hoping the buyer can run the company like it seemed that they could.

In this case, the transaction worked out well. The buyer was happy, and our client was able to maintain a large portion of his business while divesting some of his exposure.

2

Mergers and Acquisitions
The Evolution of the Laboratory Industry and Its Continued Consolidation

There is no other more complicated transaction than a merger and or an acquisition. The various issues raised are broad and complex.

They range from determining

- How to time the sale of your laboratory,
- How to value your laboratory and, more important, what metrics potential buyers or sellers may be using to place value on your company, and
- The best deal structure for your organization,

to understanding

- What builds value to prospective buyers,
- Tax and securities laws and implications, and
- The differences between stock purchase agreements (SPA) and asset purchase agreements (APA).

The industries affected by this rapid activity are diverse and include healthcare, banking, gas and oil, technology, and many others. Every executive in every industry is faced with a buy-or-sell decision at some point during his or her tenure as a leader of that company. In fact, it is estimated that some executives spend at least 25 percent of their time considering mergers and acquisition opportunities, among other structural decisions.

As you will see in the chapters to follow, the strategic reasons for considering such transactions are numerous, including

- Achieving economies of scale,
- Mitigating cash-flow risks via diversification, and
- Satisfying shareholders' hunger for steady growth and dividends.

Mergers and acquisitions are essential to both healthy and weak economies and are often the primary ways companies can provide their owners and investors with returns. Mergers and acquisitions play a critical role in both sides of this cycle, enabling strong companies to grow faster than their competition and providing entrepreneurs with rewards for their efforts. This ensures that weaker companies are quickly swallowed up or made irrelevant through insolvency or continued share erosion.

Mergers and acquisitions have played a variety of roles in corporate history, ranging from greed to good, with corporate raiders buying companies in a hostile market and breaking them apart, to today's trend of using mergers and acquisitions for external growth and industry consolidation.

Successful mergers and acquisitions are neither an art nor a science; they are a process. A study of deals that close with both buyers and sellers satisfied shows that the deal followed a sequence, a pattern, a series of steps that have been tried and tested. This book focuses on conveying this process to you, the reader, as we seek to understand the objectives of both the buyers and the sellers.

To be successful, a transaction must be fair and balanced, reflecting the economic needs of both the buyer and the seller, and conveying real and durable value to the shareholders of both companies. Achieving this involves many tasks, including

- A thorough review and analysis of the financial statements, including a minimum of three years of the income, cash flow, and the balance sheets,

- A genuine understanding of how the proposed transaction meets the economic objectives of each party, and

- A recognition of the tax, accounting, and legal implications of the deal.

This chapter is designed to provide a history of the mergers and acquisitions of the laboratory industry from its inception through November 2018. The acquisitions mentioned in this chapter do not encompass all transactions during this time frame. Many laboratory transactions are done "under the radar" and are, therefore, not published.

This information is designed to walk you through the evolution of the two largest laboratories in the US and to provide a summary table of the published transactions from 2013 to 2018. We have acknowledged some of the more memorable and eye-opening transactions that took the laboratory industry by surprise.

The Origination of the Lab Industry

It's difficult to grasp that humans once tasted urine to assist in the diagnosis of human disease. This was prior to microscopy, molecular testing, and the advanced sophistication of diagnostic techniques that continue to evolve at a rapid pace. The history of the laboratory industry is the story of medicine's evolution from empirical to experimental techniques.

The national spending on clinical and anatomical pathology testing reached $96.6 billion in 2017 according to the CMS CLIA database. The database breaks the clinical laboratory market into several segments, including physician office labs (POLs), hospital labs, independent labs, and "other" laboratories.

According to the CMS CLIA January 2018 database, there are over 8.8 billion lab tests performed annually in the United States. There are approximately 6,584 independent laboratories, including Quest Diagnostics and Laboratory Corporation of America. There were 122,131 physician office labs (POLs), with over 9,062 hospital-based laboratories. The remaining 13.7 percent of the testing volume is representative of "other" and consists of ambulatory surgery centers, ancillary test sites, assisted living, blood banks, community clinics, health fairs, end stage renal disease dialysis, hospice, industrial, mobile laboratories, rural health clinics, tissue banks, skilled nursing facilities, HMO-owned laboratories, federal health labs, pharmacy-based labs, student health services, and other laboratories.

The two largest US-based laboratories are Laboratory Corporation of America and Quest Diagnostics. Though there has been significant consolidation over the last two decades, the laboratory industry remains fragmented with many laboratory competitors in the US. These competitors consist of several national, international, and regional laboratories. Let us start by reviewing the merger and acquisition history that formed the two largest laboratories in the US.

The Evolution of Laboratory Corporation of America

One of the first companies to recognize that the industrial manufacture of medicine would be a major advance in the fight against disease was Hoffmann-La Roche. They began operations in Switzerland in 1896 and entered the United States in 1905 by acquiring County Research Laboratory.

In 1969, Biomedical Laboratories was founded. Thomas Edward Powell III and his twin brother, Dr. James B. Powell, formed Biomedical Laboratory in a hospital basement in Burlington, North Carolina. This would later be known as Biomedical Reference Laboratories. In 1982, Hoffmann-La Roche acquired Biomedical Reference Laboratories. In 1983, Hoffmann-La Roche merged all of their laboratories into one entity and became Roche Biomedical Laboratories (RBL).

Concurrently, in 1971 Revlon, Inc., a diversified manufacturer of cosmetics and ethical drugs, purchased a small clinical laboratory business called DCL BioMedical, Inc. That same year, Revlon changed the name to DCL Health Laboratories, Inc., the predecessor to the company that would later become known as National Health Laboratories (NHL). In 1994, National Health Laboratories further broadened their testing capabilities by acquiring the sixth largest clinical laboratory at that time, Allied Clinical Health. By the mid-1990s, NHL and RBL were two of the largest clinical, paternity, and drug screening laboratories in the US.

In 1995, Laboratory Corporation of America was created when NHL and RBL merged to become one of the largest clinical lab providers in the world. The company began trading under the new ticker symbol LH. The merged company created revenues of $1.7 billion USD. Today, Laboratory Corporation of America is the largest clinical laboratory in the US with 2017 year end revenues of $10.21 billion. This includes the clinical laboratory and Clinical Research Organization (CRO) divisions.

Laboratory Corporation of America, more commonly known as LabCorp, is an American S&P 500 company headquartered in Burlington, North Carolina. It operates one of the largest clinical laboratory networks in the world, with a US network of thirty-six primary laboratories. Laboratory Corporation of America performs its largest volume of specialty testing at its Center for Esoteric Testing in Burlington.

Laboratory Corporation of America was an early pioneer of genomic testing, using polymerase chain reaction (PCR) technology at its Center for Molecular Biology and Pathology in Research Triangle Park, North Carolina, where it also performs other molecular diagnostics. In addition, they perform oncology testing, human immunodeficiency virus (HIV) genotyping, and phenotyping.

Laboratory Corporation of America operates the National Genetics Institute, Inc., (NGI) in Los Angeles, California, which develops PCR testing methods. Laboratory Corporation of America's ViroMed facility, originally in Minnetonka, Minnesota, is now housed in Burlington, North Carolina, and performs real-time PCR microbial testing using laboratory-developed assays.

Laboratory Corporation of America provides testing in Puerto Rico and outside of the United States in three Canadian provinces.

Several of the more notable acquisitions throughout the last two decades that contributed to Laboratory Corporation of America's rapid growth include these:

- 2000—Los Angeles–based National Genetics Institute for an undisclosed amount.

- 2000—San Diego–based Pathology Medical Laboratories for an undisclosed amount. Laboratory Corporation of America surpassed revenues of $1.9 billion USD with over 18,000 employees.

- 2001—Path Lab Holdings, Inc., the largest regional laboratory in New England. Several weeks later, they acquired Minneapolis-based ViroMed, Inc., which specialized in clinical diagnostic testing in virology, molecular biology, serology, microbiology, mycology, and mycobacteriology, as well as in tissue and eye bank testing, for an undisclosed amount.

- 2002—Canadian Medical Laboratory Services company Dynacare, Inc., for $480 million.
- 2003—Dianon Systems, a laboratory focused in the areas of uropathology, dermatopathology, and gastrointestinal pathology for $598 million in cash.
- 2005—Esoterix for $150 million in cash from private equity firm Behrman Capital.
- 2005—US Labs, a laboratory specializing in esoteric oncology testing across multiple methodologies.
- 2006—Litholink Corporation, a kidney stone analysis laboratory.
- 2007—Tandem Labs, a Contract Research Organization (CRO), specializing in advanced mass spectrometry, immune analytical support, pharmacokinetics, and pharmacodynamics, headquartered in Salt Lake City, Utah, for an undisclosed amount.
- 2009—San Francisco–based Monogram Biosciences, a diagnostic laboratory specializing in HIV resistance testing, for $155 million, including debt.
- 2010—Santa Ana, California–based Westcliff Medical Laboratory for an undisclosed amount.

- 2010—Genzyme Genetics, formerly a division of Genzyme, with nine testing laboratories and approximately 1,900 employees, for $925 million in cash.

- 2011—Canadian central labs partner Clearstone from investment firm Czura Thornton for an undisclosed amount, thus adding Clearstone's global network of central laboratories, including sites in China, France, Singapore, Canada, and the central laboratory protocol management system APOLLO CLPM to their portfolio.

- 2011—90 percent of the shares of DNA testing company Orchid Cellmark for $85 million and, subsequently, sold parts of Orchid's paternity business to DNA Diagnostics Center.

- 2012—Laboratory Corporation of America clinical trials sold its European biological sampling kit building operation located in Hamburg to clinical supply chain solutions provider Marken.

- 2012—Medtox Scientific for $241 million.

- 2013—MuirLab, the clinical laboratory outreach business, from John Muir Health.

- 2013—Sepa Laboratory for an undisclosed amount.

- 2013—Bendiner Schlesinger for an undisclosed amount.

- 2013—Genesis Clinical Laboratory Outreach Business for an undisclosed amount.

- 2014—LipoScience, a developer of diagnostic tests based on nuclear magnetic resonance technology measuring heart disease risk for $85.3 million.

- 2014—Bode Technology Group, Inc., a provider of forensic DNA analysis, DNA collection products, and relationship testing, from SolutionPoint International, Inc., for an undisclosed amount.

- 2014—Terre Haute Medical Laboratory/MedLab, Inc., for $10.5 million.

- 2014—Covance Genomics Molecular Lab for an undisclosed amount.

- 2014—Laboratory Partners, Talon Division for $11.9 million.

- 2015—Covance, Inc., for $6.1 billion.

- 2015—Physicians Reference Laboratory for an undisclosed amount.

- 2016—Torrance, California-based laboratory firm Pathology, Inc., a provider of expertise in reproductive FDA donor testing and anatomic, molecular, and digital pathology services, for an undisclosed amount.

- 2016—ClearPath Diagnostics, a provider of laboratory diagnostic services in the northeastern United States, from private equity firm Shore Capital Partners for an undisclosed amount.

- 2016—Sequenom, a leader in non-invasive prenatal testing (NIPT), women's health, reproductive testing, and other services for $379 million.

- 2016—Center for Disease Detection for $115 million.

- 2016—Nebraska LabLinc for an undisclosed amount.
- 2016—Henry Newhall Mayo Outreach Laboratory for an undisclosed amount.
- 2017—Chiltern, a Contract Research Organization (CRO), for $1.2 billion.
- 2017—ChromaDex food testing laboratory for $7.5 million.
- 2017—Hooper-Holmes Canada for an undisclosed amount.
- 2017—Mount Sinai Outreach Laboratory for an undisclosed amount.
- 2017—Florida-based Vista Clinical Diagnostics for an undisclosed amount.
- 2018—PAML/PacLab Network Laboratories for an undisclosed amount.
- 2018—PAML Kentucky Lab Services for an undisclosed amount.
- 2018—Sciformix Corporation for an undisclosed amount.

The Evolution of Quest Diagnostics

The second largest clinical laboratory in the US is Quest Diagnostics, having a history dating back to 1967.

In 1967, Paul A. Brown founded Metropolitan Pathology Laboratory, Inc., in New York. In 1969, the name of the laboratory was changed to MetPath, Inc. MetPath was acquired in 1982 by what was then known as Corning Glass Works and subsequently renamed Corning Clinical Laboratories.

In 1996, Quest Diagnostics became an independent company as a spinoff from Corning. Quest Diagnostics is a Fortune 500 American company providing clinical laboratory services with headquarters in Secaucus, New Jersey. Founded in 1967 as Metropolitan Pathology Laboratory, Inc., it became an independent corporation with the Quest name on December 31, 1996.

In addition to the United States, Quest Diagnostics has operations in the United Kingdom, Mexico, Brazil, Puerto Rico, and India. They have collaborative agreements internationally with various hospitals and clinics. The company has approximately 44,000 employees, generates more than $7 billion in revenue, and offers access to diagnostic testing services for cancer, cardiovascular disease, infectious disease, and neurological disorders.

The following acquisitions are noted on the Quest Diagnostics website and in various industry reports including *Lab Economics* and *The Dark Report*, and occurred over the last two decades:

- 1997—The clinical division of Diagnostic Medical Laboratory, Inc., (DML) in Branford, Connecticut.

- 1999—SmithKline Beecham Clinical Laboratories.

- 2001—Ohio-based MedPlus, Inc., a healthcare technology company.

- 2002—Virginia-based American Medical Laboratories, Inc., (AML) and LabPortal, Inc., for $500 million in cash.

- 2003—California-based Unilab Corporation in a transaction valued at $800 million.

- 2005—Kansas-based LabOne, Inc., for $934 million.

- 2006—Virginia-based Focus Diagnostics, Inc., an infectious and immunologic disease laboratory for $185 million in cash.

- 2007—AmeriPath (and subsidiary Specialty Laboratories) from Welsh, Carson, Anderson & Stowe, becoming the leading provider of cancer diagnostic testing services, for $2 billion.

- 2011—Athena Diagnostics from Thermo Fisher Scientific for an undisclosed amount.

- 2011—Celera Corporation for an undisclosed amount.

- 2012—All of the laboratories from UMASS Memorial Hospitals in Worcester, Massachusetts.

- 2013—UMass Memorial for $90.4 million.

- 2013—California and Nevada-based Dignity Health's Outreach Clinical Laboratory operations for an undisclosed amount.

- 2013—Concentra's Advanced Toxicology Network for an undisclosed amount.

- 2013—Converge Diagnostic Services, LLC, for an undisclosed amount.

- 2014—Steward Health Outreach Laboratory for $34 million.

- 2014—Solstas Lab Partners Group (and subsidiaries) for $570 million.

- 2014—Summit Health, Inc. for $151 million.

- 2015—Superior Mobile Medics for $27 million.

- 2015—Memorial Care Health System Outreach Laboratory for $35 million.
- 2016—Clinical Laboratory Partners Outreach for $135 million.
- 2017—Cleveland Heart Laboratory for $94 million.
- 2017—California Laboratory Associates for an undisclosed amount.
- 2017—Shiel Medical Laboratory for $170 million.
- 2017—PeaceHealth Laboratory for $101 million.
- 2017—Hartford Healthcare Outreach Laboratory for $30 million.
- 2017—Med Fusion and Clear Point for $150 million.
- 2017—Nevada-based Sierra Memorial Hospital Outreach Laboratory for an undisclosed amount.
- 2018—ReproSource for an undisclosed amount.
- 2018—Seattle-based PhenoPath Laboratory for an undisclosed amount.
- 2018—Hurley Medical Center's Outreach Laboratory for an undisclosed amount.
- 2018—Hooper Holmes, Inc./Provant Health for $27 million.
- 2018—Oxford Immunotec for an undisclosed amount.

- 2018—Cape Cod Healthcare Outreach Laboratory for an undisclosed amount.
- 2018—MedXM for an undisclosed amount.
- 2018—Marin General Hospital Outreach Laboratory for an undisclosed amount.

In addition to the two largest laboratories in the US, the following table represents the top twenty-five US laboratory companies by revenue.

THE TOP 25 U.S LABORATORY COMPANIES BY REVENUE—YEAR END 2017

NAME	LAB TYPE	2017 REPORTED REVENUE
Laboratory Corporation of America	FULL SERVICE	$10.21B
Quest Diagnostics	FULL SERVICE	$7.1B
Opko	FULL SERVICE	$908M
Sonic Healthcare USA	FULL SERVICE	$850M
Myriad Genetics	SPECIALTY	$765M
Kaiser Permanente Laboratory	HMO	$750M
Mayo Medical Laboratory	FULL SERVICE	$600M
ARUP	FULL SERVICE	$550M
Millennium Health	TOXICOLOGY	$500M
Genomic Health	SPECIALTY	$350M
Aurora Diagnostics	ANATOMIC PATHOLOGY	$300M
Sonora Quest Laboratory	JOINT VENTURE	$300M

Aegis Sciences Corporation	TOXICOLOGY	$300M
ACL Laboratory	HOSPITAL	$275M
Miraca Life Sciences	ANATOMIC PATHOLOGY	$265M
Neogenomics, Inc.	SPECIALTY	$260M
Northwell Health Laboratory	HOSPITAL	$250M
PathGroup	ANATOMIC PATHOLOGY	$250M
Exact Sciences	SPECIALTY	$230M
Ambry Genetics	SPECIALTY	$220M
Genoptix	SPECIALTY	$200M
Health Network Laboratory	HOSPITAL	$150M
Shiel Medical Laboratory	FULL SERVICE	$150M
Diagnostic Laboratory of Oklahoma	JOINT VENTURE	$130M
Regional Medical Laboratory	HOSPITAL	$125M
TOTAL REVENUE OF TOP 25 LABORATORIES—2017		$25.98B

Source: Laboratory Economics, SEC filings, Advanced Strategic Partners

LabCorp & Quest includes Clinical Lab Testing & CRO Revenue

In addition to the top twenty-five US laboratories, there have been many active acquirers over the last several years. The following tables represent the 2013 to 2018 publicly noted acquisitions.

2013 Published Laboratory Transactions

A total of twenty-nine published laboratory acquisitions occurred in 2013. Of those, there were a large number of different buyers (twenty), showing optimism that the laboratory market was a good sector to invest one's money. Laboratory Corporation of America led the acquisitions specific to the total number of published deals, acquiring six companies while Quest Diagnostics acquired four. The growing trend of acquired laboratories consisted of a mixture of specialty (five), genetic (seven), pathology (four), clinical (six), hospital outreach (five), and toxicology (two).

2013 LABORATORY TRANSACTIONS

DATE	ACQUIRER	SELLER	PURCHASE PRICE
13-Dec	Manhattan Laboratory	Genatom, Inc.	NA
13-Dec	Spectra Laboratories	Shiel Medical Laboratory	NA
13-Nov	ViraCor IBT Laboratories	Lab Operations of National Institute of Transplantation	NA
13-Nov	Laboratory Corporation of America	SEPA Laboratories	NA
13-Nov	Levine Leichtman Capital Partners	Genova Diagnostics	NA
13-Oct	Miraca Life Sciences	Plus Diagnostics	NA
13-Oct	Quest Diagnostics	ConVerge Diagnostic Services, LLC.	NA

13-Sep	Clinical Genomics Limited	Enterix, Inc. (Sold by Quest Diagnostics)	NA
13-Sep	Laboratory Corporation of America	John Muir Health Clinical Laboratory Outreach Services	NA
13-Aug	Response Genetics	Pathwork Diagnostics	$1.2M
13-Aug	Laboratory Corporation of America	Bendiner Schlesinger	NA
13-Aug	Laboratory Corporation of America	Genesis Clinical Laboratory Outreach Business	NA
13-Aug	Gardiner-Smith Laboratories	ARUP-Animal Reference Pathology	NA
13-Aug	Bio-Reference Laboratories	Hunter Laboratories	NA
13-Aug	Gardiner-Smith Laboratories	HealthTronics Laboratory Solutions, Inc.	NA
13-Aug	Sterling Reference Laboratories	Norchem Drug Testing Laboratory	NA
13-Jul	BelHealth Investment Partners	General Genetics Corporation	NA
13-Jun	Laboratory Corporation of America	Laboratory Partners' MedLab Physician Office Business	$10.5M
13-May	Quest Diagnostics	Concentra's Advanced Toxicology Network	NA
13-Apr	Laboratory Corporation of America	Dignity Health's Outreach Clinical Laboratory Operations (AZ)	NA

13-Apr	Quest Diagnostics	Dignity Health's Outreach Clinical Laboratory Operations (CA & NV)	NA
13-Feb	ViraCor	Cylex	$15M
13-Feb	Opko Health, Inc.	Silcon Comércio, Importacao E Exportacao de Produtos Farmaceuticos e Cosmeticos, Ltda.	NA
13-Jan	Ascend Clinical, LLC.	PathCentral	NA
13-Jan	Management (Selah Genomics)	Lab 21 Limited's South Carolina Clinical Lab Operations	NA
13-Jan	Access Genetics	Oral DNA (Sold by Quest Diagnostics)	NA
13-Jan	Illumina	Verinata Health	NA
13-Jan	Quest Diagnostics	UMass Memorial	$90.4M
13-Jan	Sonic Healthcare Limited	Labco S.A. Group	NA

SOURCE: SEC filings and other publicly available sources including Laboratory Economics, Dark Report, and Advanced Strategic Partners

2014 Published Laboratory Transactions

There were thirty-six published lab acquisitions in 2014, up approximately 25 percent from 2013. The total number of acquirers increased to twenty-three. The largest acquirers were Laboratory Corporation of America (five) and Aurora Diagnostics (four). The total number of pathology lab sales increased over 100 percent from prior years (eleven), and there were notably more specialty laboratory sales than in prior years (twelve).

One of the more notable acquisitions was the announcement in January 2014 of Quest Diagnostics agreement to pay roughly $570 million to acquire Solstas Lab Partners. Solstas provides medical laboratory testing services to clients in nine states across the South. One interesting consequence to this sale is that it gave Quest Diagnostics a significant foothold in the backyard of competitor Laboratory Corporation of America. The main lab facility for Solstas in Greensboro is located just twenty-five miles from Laboratory Corporation of America's main testing facility in Burlington, North Carolina.

Solstas was among a handful of privately held independent lab companies remaining, with annual revenues exceeding $100 million. Several published estimates put the annual revenue of Solstas Lab Partners in the range of $350 million. If that number is accurate, it indicates that Quest Diagnostics paid 1.6 times the revenue.

Welsh, Carson, Anderson & Stowe (WCAS), a private equity firm, was the owner-seller of Solstas. In fact, this was at least the third time that WCAS had been involved in the sale of a laboratory company to Quest Diagnostics. In May 2007, Quest Diagnostics purchased AmeriPath, Inc., from WCAS for a price of $2 billion. Just two years earlier, in November 2005, Quest Diagnostics acquired LabOne, Inc., a company of which WCAS was a shareholder. As noted earlier, the LabOne purchase price was $934 million.

Solstas Laboratory Partners was founded in 1997 as Spectrum Laboratory Network. It was owned by three healthcare systems. In 2006, Spectrum Laboratory Network was sold to Apax Partners. Next, in 2010, Apax sold the lab company to WCAS for $230 million.

2014 LABORATORY TRANSACTIONS

DATE	ACQUIRER	SELLER	PURCHASE PRICE
14-Dec	Roche Holdings	Ariosa Diagnostics	NA
14-Dec	Sonic Healthcare Limited	San Pathology in Sydney, Australia	NA
14-Dec	Laboratory Corporation of America	Bode Technology	NA
14-Dec	Eurofins Scientific	Boston Heart Diagnostics	$140M
14-Dec	Dominion Diagnostics	Aurora Diagnostics Clinical-Greensboro, NC.	NA
14-Nov	Medical Genetics Laboratory	MIRACA Holdings	$300M
14-Nov	Aurora Diagnostics	Arizona Dermatopathology, Scottsdale, AZ.	NA
14-Nov	Laboratory Corporation of America	Covance Genomics Molecular Laboratory	NA
14-Oct	Aurora Diagnostics	West Georgia Pathology	NA
14-Oct	PDI,Inc.	RedPath Integrated Pathology	$23M
14-Sep	Laboratory Corporation of America	LipoScience, Inc.	$85.3M
14-Sep	Veracyte, Inc.	Allegro Diagnostics	$17.1M
14-Aug	Medytox Diagnostics,Inc.	Epinex Diagnostic Laboratories	$1.3M
14-Jul	Eurofins Scientific	ViraCor IBT	$255M

14-Jul	NeoGenomics, Inc.	Path Labs,LLC d/b/a Path Logic	NA
14-Jul	Cancer Genetics,Inc.	Gentris, LLC.	$6.25M
14-Jul	Incyte Diagnostics	Accupath Laboratory Services	NA
14-Jun	PathGroup	Southern Pathology Associates	NA
14-Jun	Aurora Diagnostics	Mid Atlantic Pathology Services	NA
14-Jun	Aurora Diagnostics	Hallmark Pathology, PC.	NA
14-May	Incyte Diagnostics	Medical Center Laboratories	NA
14-May	CellNetix	Highline Pathology Associates	NA
14-May	American Health Associates	MedLab Nursing Home Laboratory	$5.5M
14-May	BelHealth Investment Partners	Precision Toxicology,Inc.	NA
14-May	Opko Health, Inc.	Inspiro Medical,Ltd.	NA
14-May	Senesco	Fabrus, An OPKO Portfolio Company	NA
14-Apr	Quest Diagnostics	Summit Health	$151M
14-Apr	Quest Diagnostics	Steward Health Outreach Laboratory	$34M
14-Mar	Laboratory Corporation of America	Terre Haute Medical Lab/ MedLab, Inc.	$10.5M
14-Mar	Quest Diagnostics	Solstas Lab Partners Group	$570M
14-Mar	ABRY Partners	Aegis Sciences Corp.	NA

14-Feb	PAML & CellNetix	Joint Venture-Symbiodx	NA
14-Feb	Myriad Genetics	Crescendo Bio-Sciences	$259M
14-Jan	Laboratory Corporation of America	Laboratory Partners, Talon Division	$11.9M
14-Jan	Opko Health, Inc.	Laboratorio Arama de Uruguay Limitada	NA
14-Jan	ACM Medical Laboratory	Phoenix Pharma Central Services	NA

SOURCE: SEC filings and other publicly available sources including Laboratory Economics, Dark Report, and Advanced Strategic Partners

2015 Published Laboratory Transactions

Merger and acquisition laboratory activity decreased substantially in 2015, with a total of twenty-two transactions, almost half of the total 2014 transactions. While there were a variety of purchasers (sixteen), the two largest laboratories slowed down compared to previous years. Laboratory Corporation of America and Quest Diagnostics each completed two acquisitions. Aurora Diagnostics continued a steady growth rate, completing three pathology acquisitions. The total number of specialty and pathology laboratories led the pack (eleven) in terms of the types of laboratories that were being acquired.

The largest transaction was the announcement of medical testing firm Laboratory Corporation of America's plans to pay roughly $6.1 billion in cash and stock to buy medical research firm Covance in a transaction aimed at creating a healthcare diagnostics giant.

Laboratory Corporation of America paid $105.12 for each share of Covance, with headquarters in Princeton, New Jersey. Approved by the boards of both companies, the deal paid

Covance shareholders $75.76 in cash and 0.2686 Laboratory Corporation of America shares for each Covance share they currently owned. That gave Covance investors roughly 15.5 percent ownership of the new firm.

One of the more intriguing and somewhat surprising transactions of 2015 was a classic case of the small fish gobbling up the piranha when OPKO announced the purchase of Bio-Reference Laboratories.

In June 2015, it was announced that OPKO-Health was acquiring Bio-Reference Laboratories for $1.47 billion. OPKO intended to leverage the national marketing, sales, and distribution resources of Bio-Reference Laboratories to enhance sales of its 4Kscore test, a blood test that provides a patient's specific personalized risk score for aggressive prostate cancer, as well as other OPKO diagnostic products under development.

Another interesting purchase was the acquisition by NeoGenomics of GE-owned Clarient in December 2015. Five years prior to this transaction, General Electric agreed to acquire Clarient, Inc., for $587 million, as GE Healthcare aimed to expand its capability to predict and diagnose diseases. One of the more shocking aspects about this purchase was the fact that GE had little to no experience specific to laboratory testing in the pathology sector.

At the time of the purchase, California-based Clarient provided molecular diagnostic technologies, such as markers, which provide precise information about a patient's cancer to help doctors decide on the best treatment. It also examined tissues from biopsies in its lab to diagnose cancer.

GE Healthcare had hopes of building a $1 billion business in diagnostic solutions for cancer and other diseases. GE executives believed that expanding into life sciences would boost the company's imaging capabilities and diversify GE Healthcare's revenue base. They had purchased UK bioscience company Amersham in 2004 for more than $9 billion. GE made the strategic decision to devote hundreds of researchers to finding ways to image for diseases like cancer and Alzheimer's at the molecular and cellular level.

After five years, GE sold Clarient to NeoGenomics, who specializes in this business sector. The sale price was over $300 million less than what GE had paid for the business five years prior. GE maintained 32 percent of the company at the time of the transaction.

2015 LABORATORY TRANSACTIONS

DATE	ACQUIRER	SELLER	PURCHASE PRICE
15-Dec	Shryver Medical Sales	MetroStat Clinical Laboratory	NA
15-Dec	NeoGenomics, Inc.	Clarient,Inc.	275M
15-Nov	Sonic Healthcare Limited	Adelaide Pathology Partners in S. Australia	NA
15-Nov	Quest Diagnostics	Superior Mobile Medics	27M
15-Oct	Aurora Diagnostics	Consultants in Laboratory Medicine	7M
15-Oct	GHO Capital Partners	DNA Diagnostics Center	NA
15-Oct	Cancer Genetics,Inc.	Response Genetics	13.4M
15-Sep	True Health Diagnostics	Health Diagnostics Laboratories	37.1M
15-Aug	OPKO Health, Inc.	Bio-Reference Laboratories	1.47B

15-Aug	Quest Diagnostics	MemorialCare Health System Outreach Laboratory	35M
15-Jul	Sonic Healthcare Limited	MediSupport SA-Switzerland	29.8M
15-Jul	Sonic Healthcare Limited	KLD Laboratories in Belgium	NA
15-Jun	Sonic HealthPlus	Medibank's Workplace Health & Travel Docs	NA
15-Jun	Froedtert Health	Laboratory Corporation of America's 50% stake in United/ Dynacare Laboratory	25M
15-Jun	Aurora Diagnostics	Trinity Pathology Associates	NA
15-Jun	Aurora Diagnostics	Brazos Valley Pathology	9M
15-Jun	Summit Pathology	AnaPath Diagnostics, Inc.	NA
15-May	Laboratory Corporation of America	Physicians Reference Laboratory	NA
15-May	OPKO Health, Inc.	EirGen Pharma	NA
15-Apr	Rosetta Genomics,Ltd.	Personalize DX (Cynogen)	NA
15-Apr	Roche Holdings	Foundation Medicine	1.03B
15-Feb	Laboratory Corporation of America	Covance,Inc.	6.1B

SOURCE: SEC filings and other publicly available sources including Laboratory Economics, Dark Report, and Advanced Strategic Partners

2016 Published Laboratory Transactions

The laboratory transaction activity in 2016 was similar to 2015, with a total of twenty-three laboratory acquisitions and seventeen different acquirers. Again, Laboratory Corporation of America led the pack in terms of the total number of acquisitions, completing six while Quest Diagnostics completed one. Aurora continued to acquire steadily during 2016, and several new acquirers entered the laboratory space. Notably, the number of pathology laboratory sales (eight) showed steady growth.

2016 LABORATORY TRANSACTIONS

DATE	ACQUIRER	SELLER	PURCHASE PRICE
16-Dec	DNA Diagnostics Center	Identigene	NA
16-Nov	p4 Diagnostix	Metamark Laboratory	NA
16-Nov	Sonic Healthcare Limited	GLP Systems	NA
16-Oct	Laboratory Corporation of America	Center for Disease Detection	115M
16-Oct	Laboratory Corporation of America	ClearPath Diagnostics	NA
16-Sep	Laboratory Corporation of America	Sequenom	379M
16-Sep	Eurofins Scientific	VRL laboratories	NA
16-Aug	Pritzker Group Private Capital	PathGroup	NA

16-Aug	Schryver Medical	Professional Clinical Laboratory	NA
16-Aug	Opko Health, Inc.	Transition Therapeutics	NA
16-Aug	Myriad Genetics	Assurex Health	225M
16-Jul	Oxford Immunotec	Imugen	22.2M
16-Jun	Ningbo Medical System	Atherotech	19.6M
16-May	The Cooper Companies	Recombine,Inc.	85M
16-May	Advanced Dermatology	Skin Pathology Associates	NA
16-Apr	Laboratory Corporation of America	Nebraska LabLinc	NA
16-Apr	Laboratory Corporation of America	Henry Newhall Mayo Outreach Laboratory	NA
16-Apr	Aurora Diagnostics	Pathology Associates of Sebring	NA
16-Mar	Aurora Diagnostics	Pacific Pathology Associates of Oregon	7M
16-Feb	Quest Diagnostics	Clinical Laboratory Partners Outreach Laboratory Business, CT.	135M
16-Jan	Laboratory Corporation of America	Pathology, Inc.	NA

16-Jan	Health Network Laboratory	Fairfax Identity/ Mitotyping Technologies	NA
16-Jan	Consonance Capital Partners	Bako Integrated Physician Solutions	NA

SOURCE: SEC filings and other publicly available sources including Laboratory Economics, Dark Report, and Advanced Strategic Partners

2017 Published Laboratory Transactions

The total number of acquisitions increased substantially in 2017, with a published number of thirty-two completed by fourteen different acquirers. Quest Diagnostics led the pack, despite having slowed down substantially in 2016, with a total number of seven acquisitions. Laboratory Corporation of America followed with a total of five. Aurora Diagnostics continued their steady pace of acquiring pathology groups across the nation, completing five acquisitions.

One of the more notable transactions of 2017 was the announcement of Konica Minolta to acquire US-based Ambry Genetics in a deal valued at $1 billion. The transaction was partially funded by Innovation Network Corporation of Japan (INCJ). A total of $800 million was to be paid upon closure, with an additional payment of up to $200 million based on certain financial metrics over the next two years, valuing the acquisition at $1 billion.

Founded in 1999, Ambry is a privately held healthcare company in the US, led by founder, president, and chairman Charles L. M. Dunlop and CEO Dr. Aaron Elliott. Ambry has the world's most comprehensive suite of genetic testing solutions for inherited and noninherited diseases and for numerous clinical specialties, including oncology, cardiology, pulmonology, neurology, and general genetics. They are recognized as a leader in diagnostic solutions for hereditary conditions in the United States for performing more than one million genetic tests and identifying more than 45,000 mutations in at least 500 different genes.

The acquisition of Ambry and the advancement of precision medicine mark a strategic and important shift for Konica Minolta's healthcare business. Leveraging its long history of innovation in materials science, nanofabrication, optics, and imaging, Konica Minolta has developed a comprehensive range of technologies and services in the healthcare field, spanning digital X-ray diagnostic imaging systems, diagnostic ultrasound systems, and ICT service platforms for medical institutions.

2017 LABORATORY TRANSACTIONS

DATE	ACQUIRER	SELLER	PURCHASE PRICE
17-Dec	ACM Global Laboratories	TosCo DrugScan & DSI Medical Service	NA
17-Dec	Pragmin Prognosis	PersonalizeDx	2.9M
17-Dec	Quest Diagnostics	Cleveland Heart Laboratory	94M
17-Dec	Quest Diagnostics	Shiel Medical Laboratory	170M
17-Dec	Aurora Diagnostics	CBM Pathology	NA
17-Nov	Invitae Corporation	CombiMatrix	35M
17-Nov	Avista Capital Partners	Miraca Life Sciences	55M

17-Nov	Aurora Diagnostics	CytoPath Pathology	NA
17-Oct	Laboratory Corporation of America	Vista Clinical Diagnostics	NA
17-Oct	Quest Diagnostics	California Laboratory Associates	NA
17-Oct	Konica Minolta	Ambry Genetics	800M
17-Sep	Quest Diagnostics	Hartford Healthcare Outreach Laboratory	30M
17-Sep	Laboratory Corporation of America	ChromaDex food testing laboratory	7.5M
17-Sep	Laboratory Corporation of America's Dynacare	Hooper-Holmes Canada	NA
17-Sep	Laboratory Corporation of America	Chiltern	1.2B
17-Aug	Invitae Corporation	Good Start Genetics	35M
17-Aug	Peter Kolbeck, MD.	Path Logic	NA
17-Aug	Genesis Biotechnology	4Path,Ltd.	NA
17-Jul	Quest Diagnostics	Med Fusion and Clear Point	150M
17-Jul	Sonic Healthcare Limited	Medical Laboratory Bremen	NA

17-Jun	Quest Diagnostics	Sierra Nevada Memorial Hospital Outreach Laboratory	NA
17-Jun	Premier Health	Quest Diagnostics' 33% Stake in Compunet	NA
17-May	Quest Diagnostics	PeaceHealth Laboratory	101M
17-May	Laboratory Corporation of America	Mount Sinai Outreach Laboratory	NA
17-May	Poplar Healthcare	Bostwick Laboratory	6.5M
17-May	Aurora Diagnostics	Cleveland Skin Pathology Laboratory	NA
17-Apr	Aurora Diagnostics	Pathology Associates of Princeton	4.5M
17-Apr	CellNetix	Puget Sound Institute of Pathology	NA
17-Mar	Ampersand Capital	Genoptix	NA
17-Mar	Aurora Diagnostics	University Pathologists	11.4M
17-Jan	Sonic Healthcare Limited	Staber Laboratory Group, Germany	NA
17-Jan	Sonic Healthcare USA	West Pacific Medical Laboratory	NA

SOURCE: SEC filings and other publicly available sources including Laboratory Economics, Dark Report, and Advanced Strategic Partners

2018 Published Laboratory Transactions

As we moved into 2018, merger and acquisition activity slowed substantially. There has been a total of twenty (slightly over half of the total laboratory acquisitions of 2017) transactions announced as of November 2018. This comes as no surprise, given the price cuts imposed by Protecting Access to Medicare Act (PAMA) beginning January 2018. Medicare's final clinical lab fee schedule (CLFS) for 2018, based on private-payer data, will result in cuts averaging 30–35 percent for most of the high-volume test codes phased in over several years. The cuts have a maximum annual reduction for the first three years, from 2018–2020, of 10 percent. During 2021–2023, the reductions can't exceed 15 percent per year.

Quest Diagnostics has purchased the greatest number of laboratories, with a total number of eight acquisitions as of November 2018. Laboratory Corporation of America has followed with a total of three acquisitions as of November 2018.

2018 LABORATORY TRANSACTIONS

DATE	ACQUIRER	SELLER	PURCHASE PRICE
18-Oct	Strand Life Sciences	Quest Diagnostics, "India Diagnostics"	NA
18-Oct	Quest Diagnostics	Marin General Hospital Outreach Laboratory	NA
18-Oct	Quest Diagnostics	Oxford Immunotec	NA
18-Oct	NeoGenomics, Inc.	Genoptix	140M plus Stock
18-Oct	Quest Diagnostics	Hooper Holmes, Inc./Provant Health	27M

18-Oct	Quest Diagnostics	Hurley Medical Center's Outreach Laboratory	NA
18-Sep	Quest Diagnostics	PhenoPath Laboratory	NA
18-Sep	Quest Diagnostics	ReproSource	NA
18-Jul	Myriad Genomics	Counsyl	375M
18-Jul	Sonic Healthcare Limited	Pathologie Trier in Germany	NA
18-Jun	Roche Holdings	Foundation Medicine	2.4B
18-Jun	Laboratory Corporation of America	Sciformix Corporation	NA
18-May	Genoptix, Inc.	Rosetta Genomics	9M
18-May	US Dermatology Partners	Bethesda Dermatopathology Laboratory	NA
18-Apr	MAWD Pathology	Cytocheck Laboratory	NA
18-Apr	Aurora Diagnostics	Cascade Cytology Reference Laboratories, Inc.	NA
18-Mar	Quest Diagnostics	Cape Cod Healthcare Outreach Laboratory	NA
18-Mar	Laboratory Corporation of America	PAML Kentucky Laboratory Services	NA
18-Feb	Quest Diagnostics	MedXM	NA
18-Jan	Laboratory Corporation of America	PAML/PacLab Network Laboratory	NA

SOURCE: SEC filings and other publicly available sources including Laboratory Economics, Dark Report, and Advanced Strategic Partners

In addition to the consolidation of the clinical, anatomical, and specialty laboratories, we have seen an increase in the number of hospital outreach sales and joint ventures over the last several years. While most hospital outreach laboratories have not felt the price reductions imposed by Protecting Access to Medicare Act (PAMA) and third-party payers, they are continuing to divest of their lab operations at a growing rate. The fact that the hospitals have not seen a large price cut like the independent labs have is largely due to the hospitals' private-payer contracts.

The hospitals' rates are negotiated as part of the outpatient contracts and aren't directly tied to the clinical lab fee schedule (CLFS). In addition, the Medicare rates for outpatient lab tests are bundled into the outpatient prospective payment system that went into effect in 2014. The hospital outreach laboratories that will feel the largest impact are the independent laboratories that have a large percentage of Medicare patients.

The total published hospital acquisitions for 2013-2018 are listed here.

2013-2018 HOSPITAL LABORATORY TRANSACTIONS

DATE	ACQUIRER	SELLER	PURCHASE PRICE
18-Nov	Quest Diagnostics	Marin General Hospital Outreach Laboratory	NA
18-Oct	Quest Diagnostics	Hurley Medical Center's Outreach Laboratory	NA
18-Mar	Quest Diagnostics	Cape Cod Healthcare Outreach Laboratory	NA

17-Sep	Quest Diagnostics	Hartford Healthcare Outreach Laboratory	30M
17-Jun	Quest Diagnostics	Sierra Nevada Memorial Hospital Outreach Laboratory	NA
17-May	Laboratory Corporation of America	Mount Sinai Outreach Laboratory	NA
17-May	Quest Diagnostics	PeaceHealth Laboratory	101M
16-Apr	Laboratory Corporation of America	Henry Newhall Mayo Outreach Laboratory	NA
16-Feb	Quest Diagnostics	Clinical Laboratory Partners Outreach Laboratory Business, CT.	135M
15-Aug	Quest Diagnostics	MemorialCare Health Systems Outreach Laboratory	NA
14-Apr	Quest Diagnostics	Steward Health Outreach Laboratory	34M
13-Sep	Laboratory Corporation of America	John Muir Health Clinical Laboratory Outreach Services	NA
13-Aug	Laboratory Corporation of America	Genesis Clinical Laboratory Outreach Business	NA
13-May	Quest Diagnostics	Dignity Health's Outreach Clinical Laboratory Operations (CA, NV)	NA

13-Apr	Laboratory Corporation of America	Dignity Health's Outreach Clinical Laboratory Operations (AZ)	NA
13-Jan	Quest Diagnostics	UMass Memorial	90.4M

SOURCE: SEC filings and other publicly available sources including Laboratory Economics, Dark Report, and Advanced Strategic Partners

In addition to the increase in hospital acquisitions, there have been a rising number of hospital joint ventures. Some examples include these:

- **December 2015**—Quest Diagnostics entered an agreement to manage the inpatient clinical laboratory for all seven Barnabas Health Hospitals.

- **May 2016**—Quest Diagnostics and the HealthONE System of HCA Healthcare teamed up to enhance the quality and value of diagnostic services to patients and their doctors through an agreement for Quest Diagnostics to manage inpatient laboratory operations for six Denver-area hospitals in the HealthONE system.

- **January 2017**—Quest Diagnostics entered a Management agreement to manage the routine testing for Montefiore Hospital System in New York City.

- **February 2017**—Sonic Healthcare and Western Connecticut Health Network (WCHN) announced that they entered a definitive agreement to form a joint venture to enhance laboratory services for individuals and healthcare providers throughout Connecticut. The joint venture will operate under the name of Constitution Diagnostics Network

(CDN). This new entity combines the existing high-quality clinical and anatomic pathology laboratory testing capabilities of WCHN's three community-based hospitals (Danbury Hospital, Norwalk Hospital, and New Milford Hospital) with esoteric testing capabilities offered by Sonic Healthcare USA through its Sunrise Medical Laboratories division based in Hicksville, New York, and other affiliates.

- **September 2017**—Sonic Healthcare USA and NYU Langone Health formed a joint venture named NYU Langone Diagnostics, LLC.

- **September 2018**—Quest Diagnostics and Regional Medical Center Health System (RMC), a regional healthcare provider for a five-county service area in northeast Alabama, are teaming up to enhance the quality and value of diagnostic services to patients and their doctors through a new partnership agreement under which Quest Diagnostics will provide supply chain expertise, as well as perform laboratory reference testing.

As we moved into the last quarter of 2018, we saw more sellers seeking alternative growth strategies due to the imposed price reductions of PAMA, hence, lower profitability margins.

Many of the small to midsized laboratories will continue to experience declines in profitability and will be faced with no other option than to sell or, in some cases, shut their doors. While the US laboratory industry remains fragmented, we expect to see continued consolidation, given that mergers and acquisitions will remain a key strategy for the larger laboratories to offset the loss in revenue through volume.

Our firm has seen an increase in the number of laboratories that have taken equity investments to continue operating with hopes to "weather the storm."

While consolidation of the laboratory industry continues, we expect the laboratory industry to continue its diversification into the clinical research sector, working more closely with pharmaceutical companies on clinical trials and the advancement of drug development.

If you are considering selling your laboratory now, or sometime in the next two years, please contact our firm to begin discussions about your end game and the overall strategies to begin implementing, to ensure a maximum valuation. We look forward to hearing from you at:

m18butterworth@advancedstrategicpartners.com

3

STEP 1
Prepare Your Laboratory to Be Sold

Many of our clients ask us what to expect from the laboratory transaction process once they have decided to sell their business. This book was created to take the reader through the six key steps of the merger and acquisition process to ensure a successful transaction.

The Six Key Steps of the Lab Merger & Acquisition Process

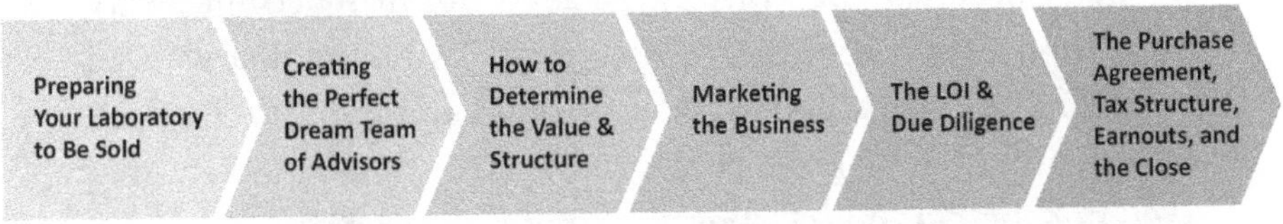

Preparing Your Laboratory to Be Sold → Creating the Perfect Dream Team of Advisors → How to Determine the Value & Structure → Marketing the Business → The LOI & Due Diligence → The Purchase Agreement, Tax Structure, Earnouts, and the Close

This chapter will focus on step one of the M&A process: preparing your laboratory to be sold. I take you through the importance of timing the sale of the business, in addition to the critical items that will need to be prepared to ensure a maximum valuation.

If you are reading this book, there is a great chance that you may be thinking about selling your business now or in the next few years. Timing the sale of your business is important, not only regarding the economic climate, but also in terms of the life cycle of your business. Here are two examples of clients we have seen over the last several years who took their companies to the market at polar opposite times.

Deal Extracts

An example of great timing: We had a client in 2011 whose clinical laboratory was growing at an annual rate of 12 percent. At the same time, a new buyer aggressively entered the market with the intent to compete against the two largest national laboratories. Amid all of that optimism, it was challenging to nail down how much growth this company would continue to experience. Our firm was representing the buyer.

We approached the owner and offered them eight times the earnings before interest, taxes, depreciation, and amortization (known as EBITDA). Could the owner have kept his laboratory and grown the company himself to realize an even bigger gain at some point in the future? Quite possibly, but it was a great exit for the seller, and there was significant risk in many of the projects that could have slowed the revenue growth. The seller sold his company and recognized a nice return on his investment.

An example of bad timing: In 2016, our firm became aware of a highly reputable cancer diagnostic company that wanted to sell. The company had been through some tough financial times and chose a brokerage company (business banker) that did not come from the laboratory industry to represent them in the M&A process. They spent the better part of a year putting together the confidential business review (CBR), while the CEO let most of the employees know that the company was being sold. He had the classic "loose lips."

Unfortunately, in this particular scenario, the timing couldn't have been worse. The company couldn't show a positive EBITDA and had experienced a downward trend in annualized revenues over the previous three years. We can explain a negative EBITDA if the owners were investing all of the profits back into the business, but it becomes harder to justify when combined with a downward trend in top line revenue.

In this instance, the CEO made the mistake of telling too many of the company's employees. In the end, the broker couldn't secure any buyers, and the company eventually had to downsize, including its sales team. Once a company eliminates the sales team, it's a sure recipe for disaster. During this same period of time, many of the company's top employees resigned, causing further issues for the company. The company ended up selling two years later for an undisclosed amount.

Know When to Sell: Where Are You in the Life Cycle of Your Business?

There are many reasons why business owners sell their companies. Several of the most common reasons are these:

- Approaching retirement age
- Burnout of one or several of the owners
- Inability to compete due to technology, insurance contracts, and other factors
- A future of decreasing reimbursements and insurance trends
- Lack of capital to expand
- Desire to pursue new opportunities
- Health issues
- Partner disagreements
- The desire to cash out

It is easy to chart out when to sell but much harder to know where you are in the business life cycle. Many M&A firm websites feature bell curve charts that illustrate the best time in a business life cycle to sell. Here is the typical chart:

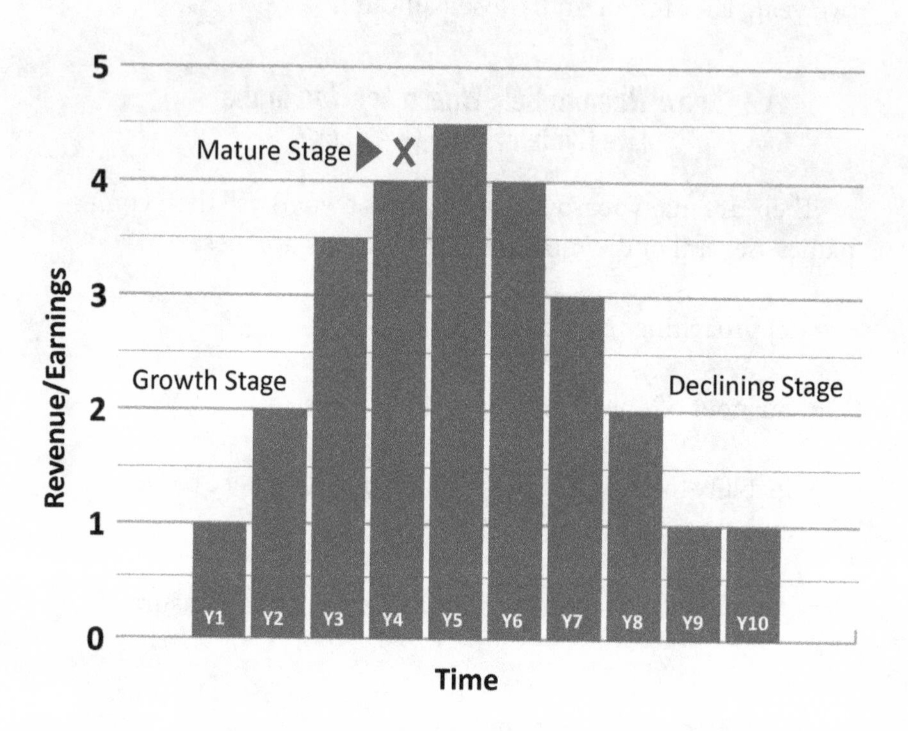

That looks nice, and it looks like it should be easy to see when to sell. It's at the X, right? Well, no. We have never seen a business with that particular curve. In many cases, the business life cycle looks more like this:

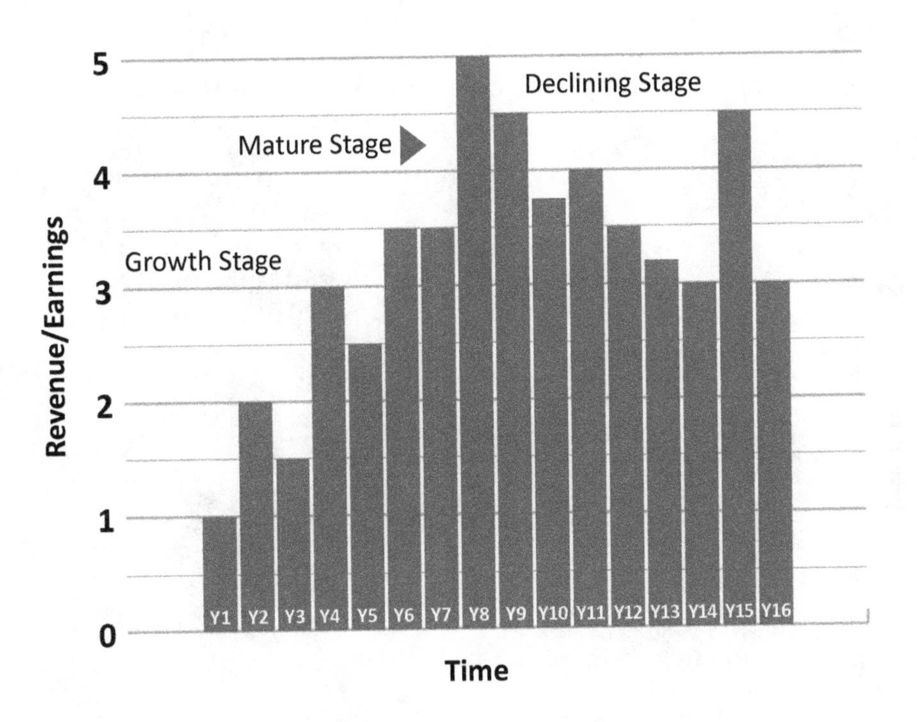

The constant fluctuations in growth, decline, and maturity aren't the only factors that will have your bell curve looking like a mountain range. One of the biggest challenges is that you can't see or predict the future. In reality, most curves look something like this:

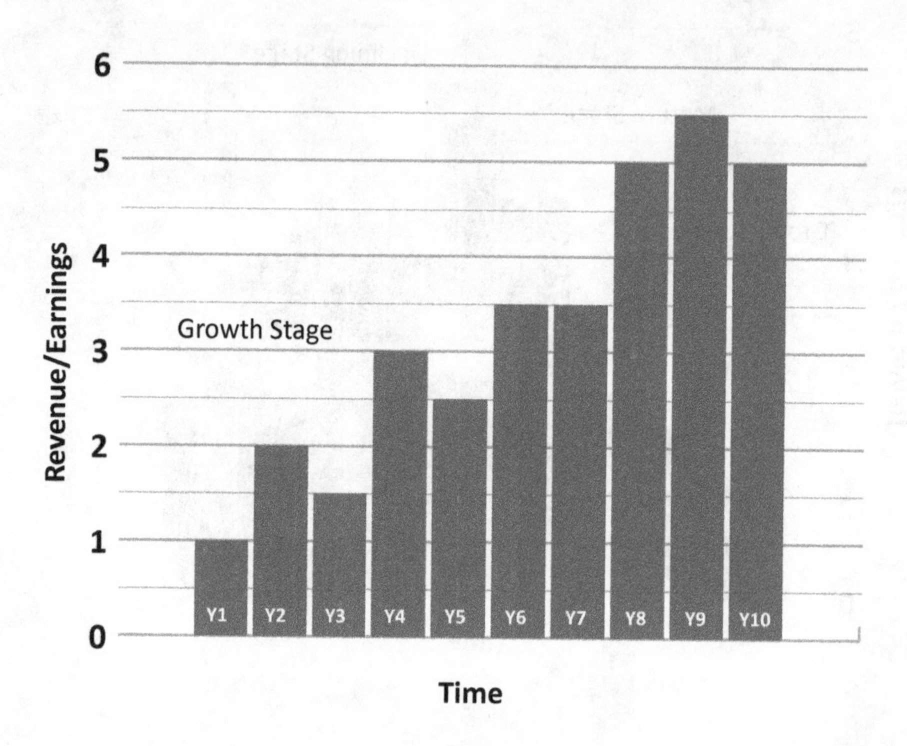

Most of us would agree that it's a bit harder to see when to sell. Is that last little dip down the beginning of a long decline? Or is it just the kind of fluctuation that most businesses will experience from time to time? Additionally, external issues can kill a business, as witnessed by the drastic reduction in reimbursement for molecular and toxicology testing in 2015.

The entire laboratory industry was being faced with price cuts as we entered 2018 with the imposed cuts in PAMA for the most commonly ordered clinical laboratory tests. We are faced with constant changes and the need to be better prepared for the future.

Externalities aside, some business owners are far better at identifying where that X goes than others. It mostly has to do with understanding your company and the market. We see a surprising number of owners who are not in touch with how their business is doing. Sometimes it stems from a simple lack of accounting controls. Other times, the owner is burned out and spending less time in the office, making them less aware of how the business is doing.

When our firm sees that a decline is coming, we will do our best to guide an owner to that understanding. We look at our job as an advisor who simply "advises" and then takes a stand back. Unfortunately, we sometimes watch the company slip into an unsellable condition, much like the example we used previously of the company that decided to sell the laboratory when the financials were in rough shape.

Once a company reaches apparent decline, they are almost impossible to sell at any price. The biggest mistake many business owners make is waiting too long before they sell. There is a saying that my greatest mentor shared with me, "Pigs get fat and hogs get slaughtered." I think at times we have all been a hog. The goal should be to learn from this and move forward without repeating the mistake.

It is likely that you will only sell your laboratory once, so it is imperative that you do it right the first time.

Timing the Sale of a Business

You may accidentally work years with little pay if you ignore obvious signs that it is time to sell your company. In some ways, timing the sale of your business is like trying to time when to buy and sell a stock. Although it can be hard to guess which market trends will affect your business, sometimes it can be obvious.

The lab industry has had a specific life cycle that has what we call growth spurts. M&A global activity during 2010–2011 had reached a significant peak in terms of sheer number of transactions, valuation, and revenue. During this same time frame, the laboratory industry saw one of these growth spurts when a new and active buyer entered the laboratory space.

Deal Extract

We will call this particular buyer BOM, which stands for buyer on a mission. BOM had one mission, and that was to buy as many labs as possible, increase their revenues, and sell to one of the larger national labs. BOM was backed by a well-known equity investment firm that had a successful run in the lab industry during two previous times. We were fortunate enough to be able to represent the buyer in some of the potential transactions.

One of the potential sellers for our buyer was a lab we will call Exodus. Lab Exodus was a reputable laboratory that had two lab owners. They had achieved many awards and had a stellar reputation. We invited the two lab owners to the corporate headquarters of our client to discuss the possibility of putting together a transaction. We knew that the fit was perfect for both parties.

Unfortunately, this was one of those cases where the two lab owners didn't see eye-to-eye. One of the lab owners wanted to create an anatomical pathology division to their existing clinical lab business. He was convinced that they could become as big as the two largest labs. He had a vision that was much bigger than what we believed could be achieved without substantial financial investments.

Needless to say, they did not sell to our client. They continued building their lab into several additional states. This is one of those stories that had a happy ending, for some. The happy ending didn't come without a lot of hard work and many ups and downs over the next six years. Perhaps it was unnecessary grief or maybe just a part of a bigger picture plan that would unfold at a later date.

A business owner who hangs on to his or her business for too long often loses far more value from the business than he or she makes in salary during that time. You can think of this as working for free.

For example, say a business is making $10 million in earnings per year, and the enterprise value multiple is six times the earnings at that point in time, so the value is roughly $60 million. The owner burns out, starts going on extended trips, and doesn't pay attention to the company. Within three years, earnings decline to $8 million, and he decides to sell. He took out half a million during those three years, but the company is now worth five times (or even less), or $40 million. Multiples are lower for lower earnings, especially for those in decline. He just worked for three years, taking out a total of $1.5 million in salaries while losing over $20 million in value. In fact, the company will be more challenging to sell because the earnings are on a decline.

Timing the sale to hit the company's peak value is always difficult, so it is best to watch for signs of trouble and act accordingly. It's better to sell a little early than too late. On Wall Street, they say, "Bulls make money and bears make money, but pigs get slaughtered." Getting greedy and trying to time the sale to squeeze as much money out of your business could backfire.

Burned Out?

Often, new ownership can interrupt the business life cycle curve and breathe new growth into a company, as shown in the graph that follows.

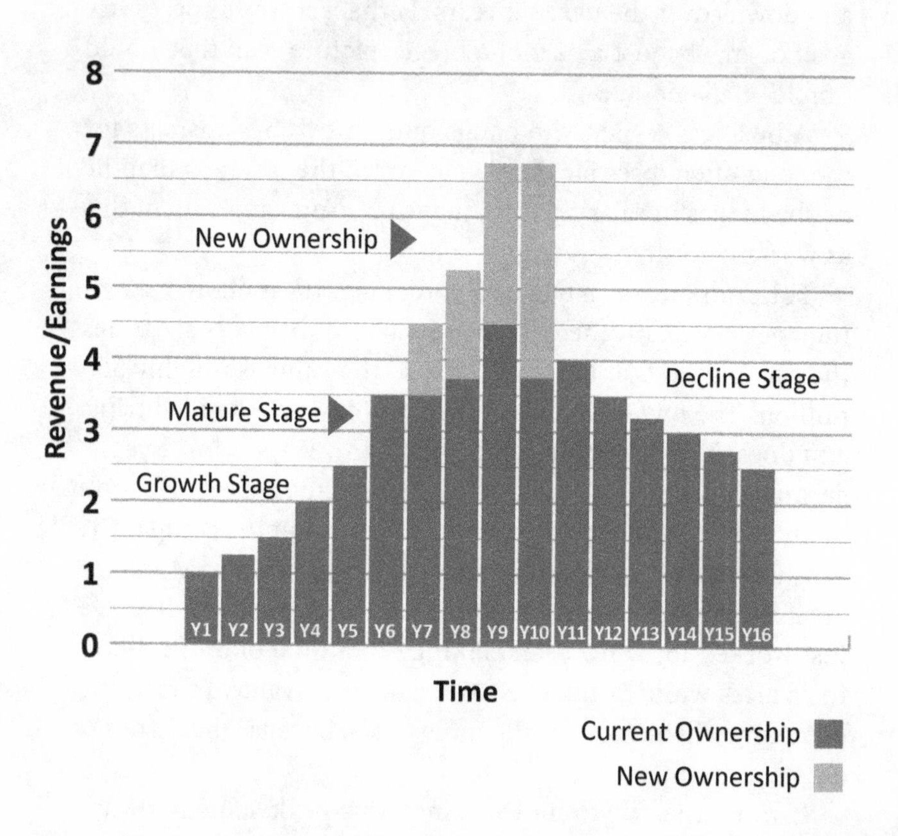

We received a thank you call the other day from a seller's wife who shared with us all of the new business ventures that she and her family had started since they sold their laboratory. She said they were glad they had sold his business when they did. The company that took over the business after he sold it had created a new market and had grown the company substantially.

Unfortunately, it is hard to get paid for that future growth if the company isn't on a clear upward path. If the company is on a clear growth path, it is possible to set up a performance-based compensation called an earnout. I will discuss earnouts in more detail in a later chapter.

How Long Does It Take to Sell a Business?

This depends on the complexity of the business, how well the lab has the financials in order (most critical), and a variety of other factors. Since our practice focuses on small to midsized laboratories, we rarely see deals close in less than six months.

We have found that the average selling time is nine months from start to close for small to midsized companies. For companies that have their financials in order and hire someone to represent them from our industry, the average is closer to six months. If the business owner has unrealistic expectations, then the business can sit on the market for a long time and potentially never sell.

Deal Extract (Example Time Line)

Day One—XYZ laboratory contacted our firm in December to discuss hiring our firm as the exclusive broker. We asked several questions of the seller and learned that he wanted to wait until after the first of the year to start the process.

Two Months—Our firm contacted the owner of XYZ lab after the first of the year. He signed an exclusive listing agreement at the end of January.

Three Months—The necessary financials were gathered to provide an opinion of value. It took a few weeks because there was an issue of cash vs. accrual accounting. XYZ lab was growing, and the owner had been using cash accounting until eleven months prior. To provide a good opinion of value, we needed a good estimate of earnings using accrual accounting, which took time.

Four Months—We met with XYZ lab's owner, presented our analysis, and provided a company presentation of our process and opinion of value.

Five Months—During the initial information-gathering phase, it became apparent that it was going to be a challenge to get data from our client. He had chosen to include only himself and one trusted employee of the company in the process. What should have taken thirty days turned into fifty days. During this time, our team completed a confidential business review document that included a complete overview of the business with seventeen exhibits.

Six Months—We made the decision to go to the market with a thorough document so that we could secure multiple letters of intent (LOIs) with a short due diligence and closing period. We implemented our marketing plan immediately.

Seven Months—The marketing campaign was implemented during month seven. The campaign targeted financial buyers (private equity) and a list of strategic buyers. We were able to secure fourteen interested parties, all of whom signed a standard confidentiality agreement (CA). We completed two site visits and management (buyer/seller) meetings. We received several letters of intent and selected a strategic buyer. The marketing process took thirty days, which was aggressive. The buyer that our seller chose to proceed with was one of the larger national labs. The LOI was specific and included an aggressive thirty-day due diligence and closing.

Eight and Nine Months—During the due diligence, it became clear that the buyer was a perfect candidate to buy and run the company. The due diligence was extremely detailed. The buyer required over 500 documents to be produced regarding the operation of the business. In our opinion, it was complete overkill that put a major strain on the seller's staff and, quite frankly, on everyone in the process. The thirty-day due diligence and closing turned into a ninety-two-day process. In fairness, a hurricane interrupted our plans and added two weeks to the process. The asset purchase contracting phase began during month nine.

Ten Months—The seller closed and walked away with $10+ million more than what he had originally anticipated and was happy to begin his new life. The buyers were ecstatic because they had purchased a reputable lab that would further increase their market share.

Selling Your Business within Two Years?

If you are contemplating selling your business within the next two years, it pays to start thinking about your tax strategy. It's simple in theory. You pay a percentage of your earnings in taxes, but when you sell your company, you get paid a multiple of the earnings as a selling price. Often, the price can vary significantly and be anywhere from four to eight times the earnings.

We have seen deals sell for as much as twelve times the earnings. This occurs in rare circumstances when a lab has a proprietary offering, specific insurance contracts that are assignable, or the timing and geographical area that the lab covers is a strategic move for the purchasing company.

Though you normally want to minimize taxes, in the year or two before you sell, you don't want to do that. You want to maximize earnings for a bigger basis to use with the multiple.

For example, in most cases you would categorize purchases as expenses, even if your accountant is telling you that you should capitalize and expense them over time as depreciation. This minimizes earnings and, thus, minimizes the resulting taxes. In a sale, the earnings used to value the company are EBITDA. Depreciation doesn't count. By definition, it gets added back into earnings. In the year or two before you sell, you want to purchase as much, say, equipment and supplies as you can and capitalize/depreciate those. It is important to discuss this strategy with your accountant.

In addition, personal expenses are written off as business expenses. We see everything from owners expensing a personal car to owners using a company work crew to build a vacation home. We can adjust earnings to reflect a stronger bottom line, but there are limits to what some buyers will accept. Too many adjustments will make some buyers nervous, and the adjustments often become a negotiated item. From the buyer's perspective, the risk goes up and the value goes down. It's far better to come clean and pay the taxes in the year or two prior to selling.

We don't like to get into a situation where the business owner wishes he or she had done some things differently in the years prior, although this happens fairly often. It's a shame because we know that they could have sold the laboratory for more if they had implemented a few of these simple steps.

A good mergers and acquisitions advisor will work with you for a year or two before you sell. The advisor will review your year end statements and identify areas where you can increase the value of your business without much effort. He or she may identify problem areas that you can work on to avoid creating a last-minute crisis. We currently have clients that we have been working with for more than eighteen months. Most of us in this industry are patient.

It is better to sell a clean business in two years than to try to force a sale of a messy business.

Ten Action Items to Maximize the Value of Your Laboratory

If you are thinking about selling your company, or a part of your company, then you must take a few steps to make your largest asset more attractive to potential buyers. This section suggests actions that should be implemented prior to selling your company so you can avoid many of the common pitfalls during the sales and due diligence phases.

1. **Prepare the business financials ahead of time.**

   Clean up the last three years of your balance sheets, cash flow statements, and income statements. It's important that your accountant has prepared clean, credible, and consistent statements that show your company's current state and track record. Make sure that your company's balance sheet has a clear current ratio. The current ratio is important because the company is considered not liquid if the current liabilities exceed the current assets. In the preparation for a sale, clean up the outstanding accounts receivables and accounts payables.

   You should consider paying off all of your long-term debt. Look into retiring the debt now or make a plan to retire the debt at closing. We have seen situations where sellers will call the lenders and explain that a deal to sell the company is on the table. The lender will sometimes take a percentage of the amount owed with terms that are more immediate for the lender. This can save anywhere from 30 to 50 percent of the debt that is owed and will make the closing easier.

Here is an example of one of the clients we recently worked with. The owner of this particular laboratory had been aggressively using the company to pay for personal expenses and wanted to make adjustments in several dozen expense categories. A business is often only worth a multiple of EBITDA. In this case, the seller had to take a lower price than he might have otherwise received. It would have been much better to start preparations one or two years before the sale.

This seller, had he produced good, clean financials and paid a few more taxes, would have sold his business for more money. It is critical to have your income statement, statements of cash flow, and balance sheets in perfect order. The minimum number of years that will be needed is three; however, we advise our clients to have the last five years. The financials don't have to be audited (privately held companies) but should be reviewed and prepared by your trusted CPA and controller/CFO. Obviously, publicly traded companies have their own standards that they must abide by.

2. **Prepare your business for a management handoff and make yourself expendable.**

Companies with the greatest value to buyers are those where the ownership is completely replaceable. The larger the business, the more preparation will be required for succession planning.

We often hear our buyers make the following comment: "We always ask ourselves, if the owner walks, does the business walk?" Ask yourself the same question. The goal is to execute a plan that would make a new buyer comfortable.

Like the financial planning, this can take a couple of years. The handoff should be clean organizationally, fiscally, and physically. It is important to begin cleaning up the sites early (such as patient service centers, offices, and laboratories).

We suggest that you train your managers to run the company without you. Empower them to make decisions and trust them to work independently. In addition to training your managers to run things without your involvement, make sure that you design systems and policies as guidelines for your employees. A buyer will want to see that you have existing policies and procedures in place.

3. **Clean up and organize all corporate documents.**

We recommend that you begin gathering all corporate documents, including leases, employment contracts, noncompete agreements, automobile agreements, policies and procedures, certifications, manuals, corporate brochures, marketing literature, payroll information, and insurance policies and upload them to a cloud-based secure environment prior to the sale of your business. We have found BOX.com to be a great service that is easy to navigate and use.

Many of our clients hire our firm several months prior to assist with this process. Our team has worked with most of the buyers in today's market and has compiled a list of all documents that will be needed to ensure a successful transaction. Most sellers are surprised at how lengthy this list can be. It is not unusual for buyers to request 450 to 600 documents. Our last transaction had several thousand pages of documents uploaded before the deal closed.

If you schedule a face-to-face meeting with our team and sign an exclusive listing agreement, we will provide this detailed information.

4. **Trim the staff and cut dead weight six to twelve months prior to a sale.**

   To maximize the value of your business, you will need to maximize the company's profits. The largest expense for most of our clients is the personnel. It is best to make a determination about what personnel are absolutely essential to run the business. This will be a time when being tough is essential. You will want to review your employees with your current management team and determine which employees aren't performing up to expectations. If you have good employees who are doing jobs that hold low value in contributing to the ongoing success of the business, try to move those employees into more productive positions.

   We recommend that you work with your advisor to evaluate your financials and perform some cross references to other companies in the industry with similar revenue and testing volumes. They should be able to make recommendations where efficiencies could be made. Most likely, your advisors will have seen similar companies in the industry that are more or less efficient. Take the time to learn from their experience.

5. **Make sure that there are no surprises; address outstanding legal and tax issues.**

   If something good or bad happens to the business, we advise our clients to let us know. Never let the buyer find out on their own. Always quickly notify the buyer of the event. The process of selling is a process of building trust between the buyer and the seller. If that trust is broken, it may become impossible to recover from, and the deal will die. Buyers want to do business with people they can trust.

   A wise business owner settles all outstanding lawsuits and is prepared to talk about those lawsuits and their outcomes. The other legal issues that commonly need to be addressed are related to any subsidiaries and companies that have been acquired or purchased during the time you have owned the company. You will need to be prepared to present all documentation.

6. **Increase sales.**

   We have seen business owners cut the sales team as part of the downsizing process prior to a sale. This is most likely the worst decision any lab owner could make. The other side of improving profits is ensuring that revenue is continuing to grow. We often witness companies lowering the sales commission plans prior to a sale. We suggest the exact opposite. It is imperative that you motivate your sales staff with more lucrative commission plans to ensure that the revenue is continuing to increase.

   One of the key areas that our team has assisted with over the years is specific to implementing new sales strategies and aggressive sales compensation plans prior to selling the business.

   This is one of several key differences in working with Advanced Strategic Partners. Our team has had continued success in ensuring that the laboratories we represent have strong sales and marketing revenue-generating programs in place.

7. **Quantify owner's expenses and other add backs to determine an adjusted EBITDA.**

   In accounting, there is a commonly used term known as GAAP (generally accepted accounting principles). Over the years, however, we have seen business owners use the MUTO approach to accounting (making up their own). Owners of closely held businesses often run personal expenses through the company books, such as family cars, travel, country club expenses, entertainment, sporting events, and many others.

If you are one of those owners, work with your accountant to determine an adjusted EBITDA. There will likely be other expenses that you may be able to add back to increase the profit outlook, including one-time expenses for legal services, severance payments, and capital expenses.

8. **Have realistic value expectations.**

Many laboratories looking to sell will not because the sellers have unrealistic financial expectations. These sellers base their price on what they need or want, not on what the business is worth. Almost all sellers can cite a reason why their business is worth more than a statistical analysis would indicate. Sellers, thinking that they will get a higher offer, have convinced us on many occasions to turn down what we would consider to be a fair offer.

We have yet to see that strategy work. The best way to handle this is to allow the market to determine the value, and to use the market to negotiate the price upward. It is essential that there is an understanding between the seller and the intermediary on an estimated market value.

If the owner has unrealistic value expectations, it would be a mistake to take the company to the market. Both the buyer and the intermediary will be wasting a lot of time.

9. **Use advisors appropriately.**

We do recommend using an intermediary, an appropriate one for your size. Get tax advice early and realize it is possible that your current CPA isn't the best person to advise you. Typically, they are not involved in M&A transactions. Have an attorney review the agreements, but remember that their only role is to advise you on contractual issues, not to control the deal. As with your CPA, your current attorney may not be the best one to advise you on your transaction. Get one with healthcare M&A experience. Experienced M&A attorneys know which points to push and which to let go. They understand what is fair and reasonable in an M&A transaction.

10. **Be mentally prepared for the emotional roller coaster of selling your business.**

    We tell our clients that selling their business will be a lot like getting on a roller coaster. There will be many ups and downs throughout the process and somewhat of a thrilling, or less than thrilling, experience. The end game is to cross the finish line together and try to enjoy the ride. All of our deals are unique, but the one explained next was a particularly bumpy ride throughout the entire process.

Deal Extract

In this particular instance, we got our seller an offer to sell his company for $10+ million more than he expected. In addition, he retained 60 percent of his company. The same seller had worked independently with the exact same buyer several months prior to hiring our firm. We often tell our sellers that they get their money back tenfold by hiring our team of experienced laboratory M&A advisors. In this case, it ended up being far greater! How is that possible? Great question.

Our seller signed an exclusive seller's agreement with our firm in January. He had worked on his own with a number of potential buyers for several months prior. Throughout the process, they had requested several documents to provide a valuation. Looking back at our experience with being able to get the needed documents to take them to the market, it couldn't have been easy for the owner to navigate through this process while trying to run his day-to-day business.

Our firm created a well-documented confidential business review that allowed prospective buyers to have a complete understanding of our seller's entire business. In addition, this detailed document was taken to the entire market, creating a competitive bidding atmosphere while adding significant value to our client's original offer.

We took the client to twenty-four of our industry contacts in June of that year. These contacts included large national laboratories, private equity groups (PEGs), and venture capitalists (VCs). Of the twenty-four contacts that we solicited, sixteen signed confidentiality agreements to review our client's operation in more detail.

Once we secured these agreements, we shared our client's confidential business review and attached exhibits. (This particular CBR was thirteen pages long and had approximately fourteen exhibits, including financials, patient service center locations, and so on.) The confidential business review is the key road map of the seller's business that is used to attract buyers. This document allows the prospective buyers to make an educated offer based on the information provided.

In this case, it took four months to assemble the confidential business review. We have the resources to put this document together in as few as thirty days, but the documents we requested were a challenge for our client to locate. Also, our client had multiple systems that he pulled reports from, and the data were not in an industry standard format.

We have designed a specific, secure, HIPAA-compliant, cloud-based environment to house all the required documents, which streamlines the process for everyone involved. I can't imagine how anyone sold a business in the good old days when today's technology wasn't available. This particular client had several thousand documents uploaded to our cloud-based secure environment by the time we closed the deal.

Our seller made the decision to work with the buyer who had made him an offer several months prior to his obtaining our firm (the one who offered him significantly more once we got involved). The main reason for moving forward with this buyer was the fact that they were willing to close in thirty days.

To get a deal completed in thirty days is aggressive and nearly impossible. Everyone was motivated and worked around the clock to adhere to the thirty-day deadline. The thirty days, however, turned into sixty and eventually into ninety-two days by the time the closing occurred.

There are many reasons that closing a deal of this magnitude takes time. In this instance, the timing issue was due to the fact that this buyer didn't change many of the internal processes to expedite this deal. In the LOI (letter of intent), they said they would get the deal closed in thirty days, but they requested the same 500+ documents that they would in a standard 120-day due diligence process.

We were able to upload all the critical items quickly, and we completed the due diligence list within ninety days. This seller did not have our firm upload the needed documents prior to taking his company to the market. We highly recommend having your M&A advisor plan this part of the process ahead of time.

Do you remember from our time line earlier that the seller decided to include one high-level trusted employee in the sales process to work with our team? We would have appreciated having the seller's CFO involved but respected his decision not to include him due to the sensitivity of keeping the sale confidential. This made our team's and his existing COO's job more difficult. Thank God our team of advisors grew up in the laboratory industry. I couldn't imagine someone who doesn't understand the lab world and the terminology trying to get through this deal. I presume this is why so many deals don't close.

Even as an M&A advisor, we can't help but get on that roller coaster with you. You can't work that hard on a deal for nine to twelve months and not have it affect you. In the end, as with the majority of our transactions, we successfully crossed the finish line together.

Key Takeaways

- Although it is nearly impossible to time the market, ask your advisor about the current state of the market and proceed accordingly.
- Be prepared for a six- to nine-month sales process.
- If you're considering selling your business in the next twelve to twenty-four months, start thinking about your tax strategy now.
- Clean up and organize all corporate documents and start uploading them to a secure web-based environment prior to taking your company to the market.
- Make sure that all pending legal matters are resolved or are easily explainable.
- Increase sales and incorporate aggressive compensation plans to motivate your sales team.
- Trim the staff and dead weight.
- Quantify owner's expenses and determine an adjusted EBITDA.
- Use your advisors wisely.
- Get prepared for an emotional roller coaster.

4

STEP 2

Create the Perfect Dream Team of Advisors

You have made the decision to sell your company and are in the process of choosing your dream team of advisors to assist in maximizing the value of your sale. Whom do you need on your team? When and how do you go about choosing your advisors?

This chapter focuses on step two of the M&A process and will focus on the who, what, when, and how to assemble your perfect dream team of advisors.

All too often, a seller jumps into the M&A process without much preparation. Before trying to sell, a transaction dream team of advisors should be brought together. Theoretically, the following professionals should be on the team:

- M&A advisor/intermediary
- M&A healthcare attorney
- Financial wealth advisor
- CPA with M&A experience
- Key trusted senior-level employees

M&A Advisor

It is essential to have an intermediary to create market competition (or at least perceived competition). Having an intermediary ensures that the price is based on fair market value, while allowing the seller to continue running his or her business.

Having the right intermediary will make the difference in millions of dollars to a seller. Remember our seller who got an offer of more than $10 million more from the same buyer five months after retaining our firm? An experienced intermediary knows when to push the buyer, when he or she is being unreasonable, and when the offering is at its maximum amount. In addition, the intermediary can play the bad cop and leave you in the position to play the good cop. We can say the things that you would like to say but should not.

The M&A advisor serves many functions throughout the process:

- Preparing your company to be sold prior to going to the market. This includes a review of the financials, contracts, and leases. The advisor will ensure that all corporate documents are prepared and centralized into one secure area.

- Reviewing the financials and providing a probable valuation. The market will dictate the price, though an experienced intermediary who comes from the laboratory industry should advise you on the most likely value.

- Creating teasers and executive summaries to gain interest from buyers or sellers.

- Contacting all possible sellers or buyers.

- Executing the confidentiality agreements.

- Preparing the confidential business review, or "the book."
- Soliciting the indication of interest.
- Conducting management meetings.
- Reviewing the letters of intent.
- Assisting with the coordination of the due diligence process.
- Coordinating the circulation of the draft purchase agreement and ensuring no unnecessary delays between both sets of attorneys.
- Assisting in the negotiations and drafting of the transition services agreement. This document spells out the responsibilities of each party and what the deal will look like post-transaction (in other words, what employees will be retained, who pays for these employees and their benefits during this time frame, what patient service centers will be maintained or shut down, who will run the testing and for what time frame, what will be communicated to the employees, customers, and others).
- Ensuring that the deal crosses the finish line and that the money shows up in your bank account.

Transaction/Deal Attorney

Having an attorney with some empathy for the business owner is helpful. We have dealt with some seemingly cold, hard attorneys who fail to listen to the goals and desires of the business owners. Some will "run off" with the deal to engage in an impressive battle with the other side's attorney, pushing points that they feel are important but disregarding the client's priorities. On the other hand, we have had excellent collaborative relationships with attorneys who took direction from the client.

It is important that your attorney has done more than one or two healthcare M&A deals. Attorneys with little healthcare M&A experience have trouble understanding what is standard for healthcare M&A business transactions. It doesn't help the situation when an inexperienced attorney gets stuck on trivial issues but fails to identify valid risks. It may be difficult to locate an attorney who has expertise in the laboratory industry. Your advisor will likely know several law firms to recommend.

Bringing in a new deal attorney can be difficult because many business owners have trusted attorneys who have become friends. In several instances where we had that situation, we were able to successfully split the work. The original attorney took direction from the deal attorney. Having the wrong attorney will be costly and could possibly cost you the deal.

We wish we did not have firsthand experience with unqualified M&A attorneys. We have experienced many cases with the wrong attorney in place. Paying the attorney promptly every month is a costly mistake. As they approach the end of the deal, they recognize that the "gravy train" is about to end. We have found that offering a substantial payment upon completion of the deal keeps the attorney in the game.

Your attorney should be thought of as a team member, not the one driving the process. Other members of your team are your deal advisor and your tax advisor. Sometimes, an aggressive attorney can hijack the process, which can cost both time and money. Remember that the attorney works for you. Try to keep an overall view of the transaction and your goals.

We recommend that you retain your attorney when you hire your intermediary. It is important to make the introductions in the beginning of the process when you have decided to sell your business. Your attorney won't begin his or her job until you have several LOIs. Behind the scenes, you will want your attorney to ensure that you have no outstanding legal issues pending. Any legal issues should be put to rest prior to the process or at least be explainable to a potential buyer.

Financial Wealth Advisor

We recommend that our clients hire an experienced financial wealth advisor. Financial advisors (FAs) are somewhat like M&A advisors in that they will gladly spend time with you, even years before a liquidity event, hoping that they will be able to help you when the deal closes. They can recommend alternative ways to divert or delay paying taxes when your money comes in.

I know many business owners feel that meeting with an FA is like counting their chickens before they are hatched. It is worth the time, however, to create an investment strategy prior to cashing out of your business.

Many different financial advisors are in the market. Some are focused on growing wealth with more aggressive strategies. Others have wealth preservation as their main goal and focus on diversification and lower-yielding, but safer, investments. It is a good idea to interview several of them.

CPA

Your CPA will be involved with many aspects of the deal. Their first job will be to produce financial statements that are current and ready for review by the deal team. They may work with your intermediary to get a valuation or perform a financial analysis. Your CPA, however, often does not see enough business valuations to do a credible job of valuing a business. Many have a book or two on the shelf, but often that creates a figure that doesn't represent the probable selling price.

Good solid financial statements are needed to properly present the business to a buyer. Audit-level financial statements are not required. We prefer to see reviewed financial statements before proceeding with our process. Getting the financial information in order is often one of the longest delays that prevents us from taking a company to the market in a timely manner. Get your financial reporting and statements in order and get "reviewed" financial statements from your CPA for the last three years, if you don't already have those.

Key Trusted Senior Employees

Once you have assembled your external group of advisors to guide you through the transaction of selling your business, it is crucial that you assemble an internal team of key senior-level executives to work with your intermediary. This team often consists of the controller (CFO), CEO, COO, VP of compliance, and the human resources VP. We recommend having them sign a strict confidentiality agreement so they will keep the deal confidential. I discuss the importance of confidentiality in more detail in a later chapter.

We recommend that you incorporate a bonus plan with your top-level executives for assisting you in the M&A process. This ensures that everyone's goals are aligned and that they are motivated to assist with the sales process. We have seen senior-level executives with no skin in the game (ownership) sabotage deals.

We witnessed a CEO who sabotaged the owner's company sale because he was so self-consumed in what a "sale" would mean for his career. He knew that he was being overpaid and that a sale would mean the end of his gravy train.

The reality of all M&A transactions is that success lies in the ability to diligently gather the data in a timely manner. If your internal team isn't motivated to assist your intermediary, the entire deal will fall apart.

Choose the Right Intermediary

Choosing the right intermediaries could make a difference in millions.

A business intermediary is a company or person who facilitates the transfer of business ownership from one party to another. Under this catch-all umbrella are commercial real estate agents, business brokers, mergers and acquisition (M&A) advisors, and investment bankers, among others.

Business brokerage is generally regarded as working with companies that are valued under $1 million or with fairly simple transactions over $1 million. Investment banks work mainly with large companies, typically public companies valued at more than $100 million. There is a lot in between, and this middle ground can be broken down as follows:

Business intermediary and size of business earnings

Main Street business broker	Upper Main Street business broker	M&A advisors and investment brokers
UP TO $500,000	UP TO $1 MILLION	ABOVE $1 MILLION

This book is intended for companies over $1 million in earnings.

Business Brokerage

Business brokers generally deal in Main Street types of businesses, including mailing centers, franchises, strip-mall businesses, and smaller community-based laboratories. Some common characteristics of business brokers include these:

- **The majority of transactions are asset sales.** Most small company sales are asset sales (the assets are sold, rather than the stock of the company), and many business brokerage firms are not comfortable with the complexities of a stock sale.

- **They use web-based marketing campaigns.** Brokers use the web to market their listings by using the main business-for-sale websites. The higher end firms go beyond simple web listings and use other internet and web-marketing techniques. Either way, these firms generally aren't versed in the customized marketing often required for selling a larger company.

- **Relatively basic transactions.** Most small firms don't have the necessary expertise or experience to analyze and creatively structure deals that can benefit both the buyer and the seller.

- **Simple packaging.** Brokers typically use the real estate model for preparing and packaging their clients' companies. They prepare a one- or two-page listing along with three years of tax returns.

- **High volume.** A successful firm is one that requires an inventory of several dozen listings. Power brokers will have more than twenty, using a young associate to do the legwork of working with the buyers. With so many listings, a broker can't afford to spend much time with each business owner.

- **They lack strategic planning expertise.** Brokers are great at selling Main Street businesses but generally lack the skill or patience to give a company long-term, value-maximizing advice. Some firms don't like to call themselves business brokers, but a quick look at their inventory of listings will reveal what types of businesses they serve.

M&A Firms

Some characteristics of M&A professionals are these:

- **Asset and stock sales.** M&A firms are adept at structuring both asset and stock sale transactions.

- **Confidential business review (CBR) expertise.** M&A firms put together full business summaries called confidential business reviews or simply "the book," among other names. This document provides an in-depth picture of the company to prospective buyers, so they don't waste a seller's time with a lot of redundant questions.

- **Custom marketing programs.** M&A firms market to strategic acquirers and/or private equity groups (PEGs).

- **Broker and advisor regulations and licensing.** Most states require business intermediaries to be licensed, whether selling small or large businesses. Small business sales are regulated by the state's Department of Real Estate. Large business sales are regulated by the Financial Industry Regulatory Authority.

The basic difference is that a business broker usually sells the assets of a business, while an M&A firm or business banker can sell the stock. Neither the real estate exam nor the stock broker series 7/79 exams are particularly relevant to selling a business. More relevant are experience, industry knowledge, and a track record of success.

Commissions and Fees

Up-front Fees

Paying an up-front fee depends on the size of the company. The business brokers handling a small company generally don't charge an up-front fee, while firms representing large companies do. There is a large fuzzy area in between. Here is a simple guideline to explain how to figure it out.

If you are a small business with earnings of less than $500,000, you would probably approach a Main Street broker to sell your business. Brokers do not charge an up-front fee in these instances. In many states, business brokerage is regulated under the Department of Real Estate. Brokers are not allowed to collect up-front fees that are considered a part of the sales commission. If they do charge an up-front fee, it has to be for a tangible product or service, such as a formal valuation or serious marketing effort (beyond web listings). Again, if you are a smaller laboratory and use a broker, there will be no up-front fee.

If your company has $1 million or more in earnings, you will want to use an M&A firm or investment bank. In this scenario, you will likely have an up-front fee and may have to pay a monthly retainer. We have seen this vary from company to company.

In the middle ground, however, it isn't crystal clear on what is what. Business brokers may call themselves mergers and acquisition advisors, and M&A advisors may call themselves investment bankers. Some high-growth companies with $500,000 in earnings may well need a good M&A advisor because of the complexities of the business, while small regional mom and pop laboratories with $750,000 in earnings may easily be sold by a business broker with no up-front fee.

When paying an up-front fee, be sure to ask what the fee is being used for. Here are some examples of items that you should not mind paying an up-front fee for:

- **A professionally prepared confidential business review.** There is a big difference between a professionally prepared business review and a fill-in-the-blank template that some firms use.

- **Sales and marketing materials.** These include executive summaries, photos, videos, blind web summaries, and letters of introduction.

- **Marketing research to uncover strategic and financial buyers.**

- **Good research entails using many resources and can be time-consuming.** There are subscription services available to do online research of companies on both a national or international basis. These tools are valuable assets in identifying acquisition activity of buyers and sellers, dates of the acquisitions, and data on how much was paid. The annual fees to subscribe to these kinds of databases can be costly.

- **You don't want to pay up-front fees or commissions to salespeople.** Some firms pay up to 50 percent of the fee to salespeople to sign you up. The best thing you can do is to ask directly how the up-front fee and commissions work. Where does that money go, and what is it used for?

Commissions/Success Fees

Business brokers usually charge a 10 percent commission on the value of the business and 6 to 10 percent on any associated real estate. We have heard of some brokers charging 12 percent and others readily dropping a few points to get a deal, but most hold firm at 10 percent.

Some brokers will "say" that they use the Lehman Scale, although, in reality, they probably use the Double Percentage Lehman (Modern Lehman Scale). Others will charge a flat percentage of the deal upon closing. If another broker is involved in finding a buyer, the fee is sometimes split between the buy-side broker and the sell-side broker.

M&A firms, like our firm Advanced Strategic Partners, have a standard fixed percentage based on the size of the laboratory. In some instances, we structure deals to include a scale that is escalated based on what we are able to obtain for our sellers. The percentage that we charge buyers is different than what we charge sellers. There is considerably more preparation required when representing the seller side of the transaction.

Business brokerage deals usually have a clearly defined value, and a success fee is relatively easy to determine. The larger and more complex deals require the intermediary and lab owner to determine a fair commission based on the amount of work and preparation required of the advisor.

Many factors come into play when determining what to charge for advisors' services, including

- The size and scope of the project,
- Whether an up-front fee or monthly retainer will be paid,
- The amount of time that the advisor will need to spend preparing the business to ensure a successful sale,

- Determining what services the client expects to receive, and
- Determining how much experience your broker has in the industry, including his or her relationships with the buyers.

Choosing an M&A Advisor

Selling your business is likely to be one of the most important events in your life. Here are some steps you can take to ensure that you choose the best advisor.

Check references from recent transactions.

Selling your business can be a long and arduous process with some tough challenges to work through. Contact a couple of the firm's clients and discuss the following areas with them:

- **Knowledge.** Did the firm have a good understanding of the accounting and financial principles throughout the transaction? Did they take the time to learn about your business? Did they get the job done and exceed your expectations?
- **Integrity.** Did the firm act with professional integrity and give honest, objective advice? Were they willing to deliver the good and bad news during the process?
- **Persistence.** Did the M&A firm stick with the marketing and work diligently throughout the process?
- **Communication.** Did the firm's employees communicate well orally and in writing? Did they keep you informed through the process?

Marketing is critical in the middle and lower middle market.

The best price and deal structure is achieved by having multiple buyers competing for your laboratory. It is as simple as that. It amazes me how many middle-market M&A firms don't understand that—and even worse, lab owners who don't.

This is less important for small companies with a tighter range of possible values. Plus, they are local and can't afford an aggressive marketing program.

For large companies with a limited number of possible buyers, a wide-reaching marketing program isn't needed. It is critical, however, to hire someone who has relationships within the buying entities.

Midsized companies benefit from marketing because statistics show that, over 40 percent of the time, the seller didn't know the buyer prior to the deal. In the middle market, using the web and making a dozen phone calls isn't enough.

Don't rush in.

Take time to get comfortable with the firm. A quality firm will give you an opinion of value before asking for a representation agreement. There is no need to pay for anything before you have an idea of where you stand and if you really want to sell. A quality firm doesn't want a client who is not committed to the process.

Get comfortable with the deal makers.

The deal makers or advisors will be your primary interface for this long and sometimes challenging process. You want to be comfortable with them and their experience level.

It takes at least five to ten years of full-time deal making to produce the deep and broad experience to ensure that deals get closed. Does your advisor have that? Does your advisor have experience in the laboratory industry? Does your advisor have other projects that he or she is working on?

Broker-advisors do more than find a buyer.

We have clients who have been contacted or have offers from prospective buyers. They want a discount on the success fee if we sell to those companies, assuming that finding the buyer is all that we do. I wish it were that simple. In fact, finding the buyer is the easiest part of what we do.

In addition to the tasks that we do before the buyer is found—valuation, market analysis, packaging, marketing, and preparing the laboratory specific to all of the documentation that will be required during the due diligence—here are a few of the tasks that we perform after a buyer is found:

- **Deal structure guidance.** An M&A advisor or business broker has the experience to guide a seller and prevent costly mistakes. For example, a skilled buyer may offer a substantial consulting or employment agreement to a seller. At first glance, most sellers are tempted to take such an offer. This arrangement is in the best interest of the buyer because he or she can deduct the full cost in the year the money is paid; whereas, typically, goodwill is amortized over fifteen years. When you think about it, it is obvious that the cost is not 100 percent salary, but most of it is counted as part of the deal price and, as such, is deducted from other components of the deal price.

  Taking a substantial consulting or employment agreement is not a good deal for the seller, however, since the tax rate is considered ordinary income tax. Even worse, there is self-employment tax added on top. In other words, by accepting an offer for a consulting agreement, a seller is losing a significant amount in tax dollars.

The point of this example is to show that a professional can help guide a seller through the maze of deal options. This is one of many issues that come up during the process.

- **Negotiations and preventing buyer and seller breakdowns.** Acquisitions aren't always smooth, and it isn't uncommon for deals to fall apart at the last minute because of a disintegrating relationship between the buyer and seller. Intermediaries act as buffers, relaying good and bad news and absorbing the harsh first reactions that bad news may elicit. This allows the buyer and seller to maintain a stable relationship.

- **The M&A advisor has an overarching view.** The M&A advisor advocates for the client and takes on an overarching view that other professionals in the transaction do not. Attorneys are paid to point out the risk in a deal, and some, not all, earn the title "deal killer." When the deal falls apart, and they usually do at some point, the M&A advisors are often the only ones in the transaction who can stand above it all and work toward a reasonable solution to bring the deal back together.

- **The M&A advisor drives up the valuation by implementing a competitive marketing campaign.** The M&A advisor who has a successful track record of selling laboratory businesses will have relationships with many, if not all, of the market buyers. They will know the buyers' hot buttons and will be able to properly position your laboratory through a competitive marketing campaign. The single biggest reason that you don't want to sell your laboratory without an advisor is based on this concept. The marketing campaign and perceived competition are worth their weight in gold.

- **The M&A advisor will understand how to negotiate the ideal transition services agreement.** A successful and experienced advisor will assist in negotiating a transition services agreement. He or she will assist in educating your team on the importance of the post-transition activities. These critical details will be addressed in the transition services agreement that is executed at the same time as your definitive purchase agreement and other accompanying agreements and exhibits. This is often an overlooked aspect of most deals, yet it can be one of the most critical.

Key Takeaways

» Your dream team of advisors should include an M&A advisor, M&A healthcare attorney, financial advisor, CPA with M&A experience, and an internal senior group of executives to assist with the sales process.

» Check references for all advisors.

» The confidential business review, also known as "the book," will be prepared by your M&A advisor and is the main sales tool that will allow potential buyers to evaluate the details of your company.

» M&A advisors perform many functions during the sales process. The single most important function is creating market competition.

» Don't overlook the importance of a well-thought-out transition services agreement.

5

STEP 3

Determine Valuation and the Deal Structure

Once you have decided to sell, prepared your laboratory for the sale, and have assembled your perfect dream team of advisors, it is time to determine an appropriate valuation and structure.

Unlocking the mystery of knowing how much to pay for a company was one of the many reasons that I became interested in my profession as an M&A advisor. Knowing how to value a business is at the core of successful mergers and acquisitions.

This chapter focuses on step three of the M&A process: determining valuation and the deal structure. In this chapter, I will introduce you to the concept of valuation by explaining the following:

- The definition of valuation and what factors affect valuation
- Common valuation methods used
- Why buyers will pay what they pay
- How sellers can create a more compelling valuation
- Return on investment expected by strategic buyers, private equity groups, and venture capitalists
- The differences between an asset and a stock sale

Valuation is essentially the price one party is willing to pay another for his or her business. The price that someone is willing to pay boils down to what you can successfully negotiate. Valuation is the intersection of cash flow and time. The buyer will look to see how long it will take them to recoup their investment. The seller will review how many years' worth of profits they will forgo to take their profits today.

There are many factors to consider, beyond cash flow and time, when valuing a business, including these:

- Risks associated with the business contracts, fee cuts, regulation changes, and so on
- Prospects of the business sales pipeline, past and future growth projections
- Cost of capital—Can investors deploy their capital into deals that offer a higher return on their investment?
- Economic risks—This is also known as systemic risk and is essentially those risks affecting the economy.

Common Business Valuation Methods

What is the fundamental value of a business? There are a lot of rules of thumb out there for business valuations, but here are several of the more popular methods:

- **Multiples of EBITDA (adjusted EBITDA):** Valuing a company by taking the earnings before interest, taxes, depreciation, and amortization and reviewing multiple risk factors to determine a likely multiplier.

- **Discounted Cash Flow Analysis:** Valuing a company by projecting its future cash flows, and then using the net present value (NPV) method to value the business.

- **Comparable Company Analysis:** Evaluating other similar companies' current valuation metrics that are determined by market prices and applying them to the company being valued.

- **Precedent Transaction Analysis:** Looking at the historical prices for completed M&A transactions involving similar companies to get a range of valuation multiples.

- **Leverage Buyout:** This values a company by assuming that the acquisition of the company is through a leveraged buyout, which means that a large amount of borrowed funds will be used for the purchase. The funds borrowed will require a set rate of return for the purchasing entity.

Valuation comes down to how much money the business will produce in the future and the risk factors associated with generating that money. For larger companies, great effort is placed in modeling the future and then discounting that stream of cash to present-day dollars.

This can be incredibly complex, right down to calculating the discount rate to be used. Small and midsized companies also use future earnings. Since it is too difficult and risky to predict the future, we assume that the past will indicate what the future will bring. Thus, when a mergers and acquisitions firm says that your business is worth five times your earnings, there is a big assumption that those earnings will continue into the future. Everything is based on that basic assumption.

Regardless of what valuation method is applied to determine the value of your laboratory, each will require an in-depth review of additional components. This book would be far too long if we analyzed each of the methods. Therefore, we will focus on applying the more common method for small- to middle-market laboratory sales of independently held laboratories.

Multiples of EBITDA (adjusted EBITDA)

The main factor that will affect valuation is EBITDA. The term earnings before interest, taxes, depreciation, and amortization is used for middle-market companies with earnings greater than $500,000. The term is commonly used to show an investor and/or buyer what he or she can expect to earn for the investment. Simply put, EBITDA is a way for an investor to measure the return on investment should he or she purchase a company.

The average valuation range is four to six times EBITDA. The magic number in the M&A deal-making world is five times EBITDA. These numbers are known as multiples. For example, a company that has an EBITDA of $5 million would have a $25 million valuation.

Discounted Cash Flow Analysis

As previously mentioned, advanced investors go further than EBITDA and use a discounted cash flow model (DCF). EBITDA is not a true cash flow. What an investor wants to know is how much cash a business will generate in the future. A DCF model includes taxes, working capital, growth, and anything else that impacts cash flow. It then discounts those future cash flows to a present value. DCF is challenging to project precisely because it can be difficult to estimate future cash flows and to calculate a discount rate factor for risk.

Smaller businesses (laboratories with less than $500,000 earnings) are valued on the seller's discretionary earnings (SDE also known as DE). Seller's discretionary earnings is defined as net income before taxes (operating income), interest, depreciation and amortization, owner's compensation, benefits, and nonrecurring expenses. Most small businesses sell for 1.5 to 3.5 multiples times the yearly SDE, depending upon the value factors of the business. Things that determine the multiple or value factor include

- Stability of historical earnings,
- Business and industry growth,
- Type of laboratory,
- Location and facilities,
- Stability and the skill of employees,
- Competition,
- Diversification of products,
- Services and geographical markets,
- Desirability and reputation,
- Depth of management, and
- Terms of the sale.

The national average of a small business sale is 2.76 times SDE. The inventory, equipment, and fixtures are included in the price. The owner's compensation and benefits are included in the SDE. Another way of looking at SDE is to simply take EBITDA plus owner's salary and benefits. Essentially, if you take the SDE times 1.5 to 3.5 times multiple, you should have a similar number if you were to calculate 4 to 6 times EBITDA.

EBITDA attempts to standardize the earnings number by excluding items that are variable and discretionary from company to company. For example, one company may have a heavy debt load while another may have none. So we exclude interest expense from EBITDA. A buyer then calculates what his specific debt load will be and adjusts the earnings number to fit his situation. This would be the same with taxes.

Some companies have different tax strategies, so EBITDA uses a pre-tax earnings number. Depreciation and amortization are noncash expenses and are excluded.

Don't completely discount the depreciation of assets, however. A smart seller will capitalize and depreciate assets instead of expensing them in the years before a sale to boost earnings. A smart buyer will remove depreciation but then look at expected capital expenditures (CapEx) so that he or she will know that the cash flow to continue purchasing assets will be available.

Adjusting Earnings and Add Backs

The value of a business is almost always dependent on earnings. It is *adjusted* earnings, called adjusted EBITDA, that is used for the valuation. For instance, EBITDA is often adjusted to make sure it is before taxes, interest, and depreciation. Owner's benefits can also be an adjustment, which can be a tricky add back. Remember, EBITDA reflects the earnings flowing to an investor who owns a company.

We often work with an owner who isn't being paid market rates. It may be far more than market rates or far less. For example, the owner takes out earnings via dividends or simply leaves it in the business to fund growth. A fair and accurate EBITDA number includes the market rate wages and benefits of a manager who doesn't own the company. The easiest way to do this is to add back all the current owner's wages and benefits while subtracting out the market rate wages and benefits of a professional manager.

Of course, it often isn't that simple. We will see multiple owners of one company (pathologist and son team, for example) who work part-time and complete two separate work functions. How many people would the new owner have to hire to replace them? Two half-time workers? Sometimes, we see a spouse working full-time in the company and not getting paid at all. In that case, we have to do a negative adjustment to account for the fact that a new buyer is unlikely to find someone to work for free.

Other add backs for owner's benefits are health insurance, life insurance, pension plans, and any owner perks, such as personal expenses written off as company expenses. We have seen companies with six- to seven-digit charitable contributions, where their chosen charity project was a second home office for the owner. The purpose is to determine what benefits a new owner would enjoy and what discretionary expenses a new owner may decide to spend according to their own taste.

Sometimes, it gets awkward when the owner is taking so many perks that it really comes down to red flags about how they compute their taxes. Everyone does some tweaking, such as putting the family's cell phones into the company or writing off car expenses when the company doesn't really use the car. We caution owners to get their books clean early and to pay additional taxes in the year or two prior to selling.

Other add backs include

- One-time expenses, such as moving, legal, or major repairs,
- Excessive rent expense paid to a related party,
- Excessive compensation and benefits paid to the business owner, employees, or relatives,

- Excessive travel and automobile payments made to business owners and relatives,
- Bad debt expenses outside of the normal range, and
- Excessive office-related expenses.

Once you have the correct add backs folded back into earnings, you then have your adjusted EBITDA. This number can be used to compare the company to similar companies across the industry for the purposes of valuation.

Some M&A firms (and sellers) get aggressive when it comes to adjusting financial statements. Besides automatic add backs for taxes, depreciation, and interest (these are added back by definition), you can adjust for the aforementioned one-time expenses and discretionary expenses. It isn't a cut-and-dried formula, and it takes common sense to apply the rules. The basic premise of these adjustments is that you are trying to estimate what a buyer will experience in the future as the new owner. It is that simple.

If the owner of a company is doing the work of two people, then the add backs need to be adjusted to accommodate for potentially adding another employee. We have seen buyers trying to find ways to increase expenses and reduce the recast EBITDA. It is our job to ensure that the initial presentation of the financials is properly accounted for. We prefer not to have any surprises once the company has been taken to the market.

It can get even trickier if you're selling the business to a company that decides to do a straight asset purchase of the seller's client list and some of the existing laboratory or patient service center locations. In these cases, it takes a savvy advisor to assist in calculating the adjusted EBITDA. This can make a significant difference in the adjusted EBITDA and overall price a buyer would be willing to pay.

In the example with the seller who ended up with a valuation of $10+ million more for his business from the same buyer five months after he hired our group to represent him, this was exactly what occurred. We were able to identify the overlap in expenses that the two combined companies had and, consequently, were able to drive up the value of our seller's business. This would not have been an easy task for someone who doesn't come from the laboratory industry. For example, we spent countless hours reviewing the competitive landscape state by state specific to overlapping patient service centers, testing sites, couriers, and other features.

Deal Extract

Future earnings equals value. One can classify a company as stable and low risk or high growth, yet risky. In fact, this is what separates private equity (stable and low risk) with venture capital (high growth yet risky). The company that we were representing had a stable business with a diverse client base and EBITDA of $10 million. They had been rapidly growing and were beginning to invest the monies back into the company to fund the expansion of patient service centers and the opening of two additional lab operations.

The challenge was placing a value on the entire company. The core business was stable, meaning a buyer could be comfortable that those earnings would continue in the future. We wouldn't have a challenge getting cash up front for the business, except that it wasn't high growth, so the multiple wouldn't be that high, probably between four and five times earnings. This didn't take into consideration the new business that they were poised to get and had spent time and money on, yet hadn't received a dollar of revenue from. How do you value that?

We have learned not to price a company. It is best to let the market determine the value by creating market competition throughout the M&A process. In this situation, we had to spend a lot of time with the buyers discussing the two segments of the business. We discussed the fact that we would be accepting offers that included cash, stock, and possible earnouts.

Why Use Multiples of Earnings?

It is common to hear M&A advisors say, "That business is worth four or five times earnings." What exactly does that mean? We know that value is really based on future earnings. If you take a future earnings stream and discount that back to current dollars, that is like taking past earnings and multiplying that by a factor, assuming that past earnings predict future earnings.

As previously discussed, medium-sized companies (above $1 million in earnings) use a multiple of EBITDA for valuations. The multiples generally range from three to seven, with four to six being more common. We have seen multiples go as high as twelve times EBITDA, but this is extremely rare.

The valuation multiples of companies grow with size. For example, other things being equal, the multiple for a company with $1 million in earnings will trend toward four to five times EBITDA, while companies over $10 million in earnings will trend toward eight times EBITDA. In fact, you can trend the multiples right up into the large public company arena.

The P/E ratio of a public company is roughly the same as an EBITDA multiple, although the main difference is that P/E is based on after-tax earnings, so the multiple will naturally be higher. In the laboratory sector, the larger publicly traded companies have a P/E ratio of between fifteen and twenty-five.

Larger companies with an EBITDA of more than $20 or $30 million can be valued by comparing them with similar public companies. Smaller companies generally have too many additional risk factors to be able to estimate the value using this method.

Middle-Market Business Valuation

Valuation Guide and Chart

The following diagram sums up the average variation applying the EBITDA multiple valuation metric for middle-market businesses (businesses with earnings between $1 million and $20 million). The basic rule of thumb for a growing company with $1 million in earnings is a value of five times EBITDA. Why five? Simply because the average selling price for many businesses turns out to be five times EBITDA. (As I mentioned before, it is higher for companies with significantly more than $1 million in earnings).

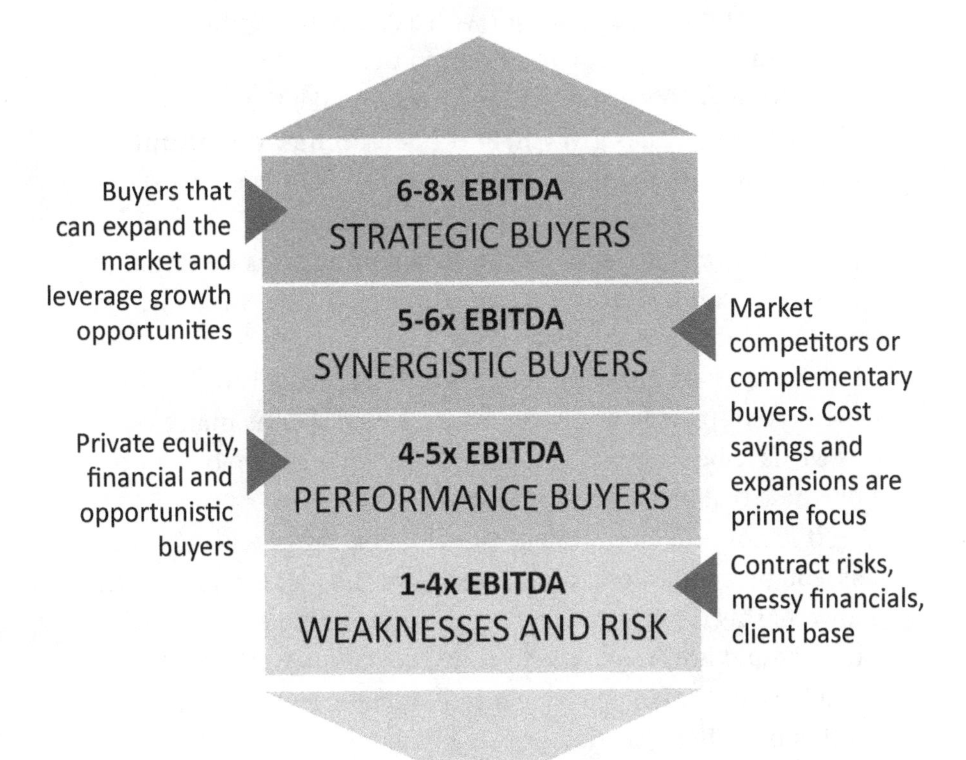

Do middle-market buyers really use a multiple of five times EBITDA when buying a business? No. As mentioned, they will perform extensive analyses and run financial models for every deal using their own internal metrics. After all the analyses and models are created and run, some deals end up below five and some above, but the average has remained around five. This also assumes modest growth.

This brings us to the valuation guide. What the chart shows is that the five times base value assumes that the company has a stable history of performance and no significant issues. A stable financial performance is the foundation and the most basic component of a valuation.

EBITDA can be enhanced by a buyer who can reduce costs and take advantage of other synergies. Therefore, the synergistic buyer can afford to pay a little more for the company. They will not want to, of course, but with a competitive situation and negotiations, the price can be driven up.

A strategic buyer who can go further, take the company to a new level of sales growth, and open up new opportunities (usually in addition to the cost synergies mentioned here) can afford to pay more. However, it still comes down to financial performance and earnings. The strategic buyer is betting that he or she can pay now for later earnings. Unfortunately, the strategic buyer who will pay a substantial premium is rare. We have witnessed firsthand that every buyer has his or her own metrics on pricing and structuring a deal. For as many years as we have been doing this, we have rarely seen two offers on a business that were exactly the same.

It is not uncommon to see a valuation range with as much as a 30 percent difference in value from the highest offer to the lowest. This is why it is important to get multiple offers and to understand how the market values the company. We say that if you have one offer, you have no solid offers. How do you know if that one offer is a good one or a bad one?

There is no perfect laboratory business out there. There are always issues, and if they are serious enough to cause a risk that future earnings may not actually turn out as expected, these issues work to pull down the valuation. Do you have one customer (or supplier) who contributes more than 15 percent of your revenue? Do you have messy financials? What about lots of adjustments to the earnings? The answers to these questions can pull that five times multiple down to a four times multiple or lessen the cash at closing. If you have a strategic buyer, perhaps they will only pay five times instead of six times EBITDA.

A professional valuator uses a similar process to this guide by taking a closer look at your fundamental performance. They will review whether the laboratory market in your area has a history of strategic buyers, and then they will discount the value based on some of the risk factors. If you can stand back and take an objective look at your business, you should be able to estimate a multiple for your business.

Why would a buyer pay more for one laboratory with similar financials of another?

Let's say that we have two companies, Lab A and Lab B, that each have $4 million in earnings for the past five years and offer a similar test mix. What could make Lab A worth more than Lab B? The answer will surprise many business owners.

Some may argue that if both companies make the same in earnings and those earnings are stable, then they should theoretically be valued the same. Quality does matter, and quality companies can demand a premium.

What does quality mean in terms of an increased purchase price? It is important to understand attributes that don't define quality, in addition to those that do. Each year, we get several laboratory owners who believe that they have a great proprietary test menu with such a great reputation that they should receive a premium valuation.

For example, let's say that Lab B has developed a specialized test for the thyroid. That's nice, but the fact is that Lab B is earning $4 million annually, partly because they have been operating with this proprietary test for the last ten years. The thyroid testing revenue is already built into earnings and, thus, built into the sales price. The only bonus a buyer gets is that, if Lab B ever shuts down, they could sell the proprietary testing to a competitor, assuming that the patent hasn't expired and that the market hasn't developed a newer, more improved test.

In other words, having a great proprietary test doesn't mean quality in terms of the purchase price. Having a great location, patents, talented workforces, and other positives about your business are already built into the earnings and the purchase price.

It all boils down to what assets are earning in profits. They will pay you for what you have done, but they will buy you because of their belief in the future potential of the business.

Seven Key Attributes that Define a Quality Business in the Eyes of a Buyer

A quality company makes buyers comfortable. A quality company is one with low risks. The following seven attributes define a quality company in the eyes of the buyer and, therefore, will likely result in a higher valuation:

1. **Clean Financials**

   There is nothing more comforting to a buyer than knowing that $4 million in earnings really is $4 million in earnings. If the owner has been overly aggressive with miscategorizing the taxes, the buyer's comfort level goes down. If the financials are messy or questionable, the comfort level goes down even more.

Buyers like to see consistency in the financials. We advise having three to five years of cash flow, income statements, and balance sheets in perfect order. You will need to have your taxes current and readily available.

2. **Solid Management Team**

   Buyers focus on the continuity of the business, and management plays a key role in that. Is the business dependent on the owner? Is the owner staying? Is there a management team in place if the owner is leaving? If all of the pieces are not in place, buyers start to feel uncomfortable. Buyers will pay a premium for a business that has built a solid management team and that is not heavily dependent on the owner.

3. **Diversified Client Mix**

   Are the customers committed to buying in the future? Is any single customer responsible for more than 15 percent of the overall revenue? Are customers good at paying in a timely manner? Could a new owner expand the relationships with the current customer base? Strategic buyers are frequently motivated to acquire based on the answers to these questions.

4. **Solid Future Earnings**

   A smart buyer will validate the $4 million in historical earnings over three to five years but focuses on the future. Take a close look at historical growth rates, market trends, life stages of the company's service lines, and other measures. Anything that can make the buyer feel comfortable that the $4 million in earnings is sustainable and can grow will move the company into the quality territory.

   The opportunity for the future and the buyer's ability to tap into that potential will be directly reflected in the price they pay. That is why it is important to identify the value drivers of the business and to spend a lot of time talking about future growth potential.

5. **Strategic Locations and Key Insurance Contracts**

If your laboratory is located in a strategic part of the country where the buyer does not currently have existing operations, this could constitute a quality opportunity. In addition, if your business is in a geographically desirable location for healthcare, including the payer mix, contracts, and reimbursement rates, this could increase the value. If you have certain key insurance contracts that are assignable to a new owner, this will increase the value.

Perhaps your laboratory is located in an area that the buyer already has a main testing facility. This may present an opportunity to structure a simple asset sale and increase the seller's adjusted EBITDA due to immediate economies of scale. All of these factors come into play when looking at the valuation of your business.

6. **Compliant**

Showing a history of compliance with a laboratory's billing practices is critical. This includes showing policies and established practices that outline how the company handles copays, deductibles, out of network charges to insurance companies, clients, and patients. In addition, all compliance manuals and inspections need to be accounted for and presented. A laboratory that has a history of well-documented practices increases the value.

7. **All of the Above**

Although we have said that a proprietary test or a talented team doesn't matter, they do when taken together. A quality company has several characteristics that, when considered alone, won't increase the value. Together, these characteristics cause a buyer to say, "There isn't a lot to worry about with this company. I can imagine owning this." The purchase price of the business still comes down to future earnings, but with a quality company, those earnings have less risk associated with them.

Less Risk = Premium Multiple

Return on Investment Expected by Strategic Buyers, Private Equity Groups, and Venture Capitalists

Return on investment, or ROI, is the most common profitability ratio. There are several ways to determine ROI, but the most frequently used method is to divide net profits by total assets. If the net profit is $100,000 and your total assets are $300,000, then your ROI would be 33 percent.

A venture capitalist typically seeks a 50 percent return per year. The return on investment that a private equity group seeks is between 25 and 35 percent. The ROI that large companies look for is somewhere between 8 and 10 percent. The difference often takes business sellers and M&A firms by surprise, but it makes perfect sense when you take risk into account.

Return on investment (or return on equity) is a method of measuring that payback and involves forecasting the cash flow of the acquisition compared with the initial investment and calculating the rate of return.

Large companies generally have a low cost of capital. They can raise money by selling stock or using debt. An average of these sources is called the weighted average cost of capital, or WACC. When a company looks at a possible acquisition, the rate of return to the internal cost of raising money will be evaluated. This is the WACC.

If a project returns more than the WACC, it is considered a good investment since the company can make more money with the project than it costs to get the money.

The amount of risk raises the required ROI significantly. As mentioned, private equity groups (PEGs) require 25 to 35 percent per year return on their investment. Interestingly enough, this often equals about a five times multiple of EBITDA. PEGs invest in mature, relatively stable, profit-generating companies. Venture capitalists (VCs) invest in early stage, often pre-revenue companies.

The difference is the risk. In fact, trained business appraisers will "build up" the discount rate (essentially ROI) used for valuations. They'll start with the low-risk discount rate, similar to what a large, stable company uses, and add risk premiums.

There are significant risk premiums added just by the fact that a company is small. In some high-risk laboratory specialties (such as toxicology), they end up with a 50 percent discount rate after all of the risk factors are added back in.

That discount rate is applied to future estimated cash flow. A high-risk toxicology laboratory with huge future potential cash flow will be discounted heavily because of the risk premium associated with that specialty. It may make sense when viewed as an entire portfolio. Some toxicology laboratories have had enormous payoffs, but most don't. The high fliers cover the losers, so the portfolio still makes a positive return. By requiring a 50 percent ROI, the venture capitalist ensures that the upside is possible.

Private equity groups have an interesting multilayer business model. They generally raise money from wealthy individual investors or institutional investors (or larger PEGs) and frequently try to produce an ROI of 15 to 20 percent for these investors. However, they seek opportunities that produce 25 to 35 percent on their investment. The difference, of course, is how the PE fund managers make their money. Some managers will charge an annual management fee or a deal origination fee. Their success is measured by the return that they make for their investors.

Typically, PEGs try to exit an investment in three to seven years, although some funds will hold longer. Some have specific timelines that they have advertised to their investors, and these funds definitely feel pressure to exit a business at the end of a fund's life. If successful (the fund investors realize 15 to 20 percent return on investment), then the fund managers are more likely to be able to raise money for future investments. If they are not successful, then they risk not being able to raise additional money and having to exit the private equity market.

How to Sell an Unprofitable Laboratory

Not all companies make the decision to sell during the rosiest of circumstances. Sometimes sellers need to unload debt-laden or money-losing businesses. Selling these companies is trickier than finding financing for healthy companies, but it's not impossible. Debt is greater than purchase price when the external debt of a business exceeds the purchase price that a buyer is willing to pay, which is known as being underwater. In this situation, the seller has a couple of options for selling the company:

- **Ask the buyer to pay more.** The seller should explain the situation to the buyer; if the buyer is hot enough for the deal, they may be willing to pay enough to cover all the outstanding costs and debts of the business.

- **Negotiate with the creditors.** This situation is tricky because informing a creditor that a company is in financial trouble may cause that creditor to place a lien on the business or force a bankruptcy. The key is to let the creditor know that he or she will get something. If the seller in financial straits can get major creditors to agree to accept less than the full amount owed, then the seller may be able to extract themselves from this precarious position without having to bankrupt the business.

Buyers of troubled companies shouldn't let sellers repay all creditors. Instead, buyers should take complete control of the situation. Buyers should have the sellers submit a complete list of all the business's creditors and directly pay all outstanding debt of the business at closing.

- **Determine the contribution.** Determine the revenues minus direct costs associated with those revenues (typically the cost of goods sold, salespeople, marketing, and so on). For example, let's say that the seller has $30 million in revenue and $32 million in costs, resulting in $2 million in losses. Assume the direct costs associated with those revenues is $22 million. Therefore, the total non–sales-and-marketing administrative costs are $10 million ($32 million minus $22 million). In this example, the seller would provide $8 million in contribution ($10 million minus $2 million = $8 million) to the buyer, assuming the buyer has sufficient existing administrative overhead to absorb without needing the seller's full $10 million of non–sales-and-marketing administrative costs.

  In this example, the question that the seller should ask the buyer is "What value does my company's $30 million in revenue and $8 million in contributions have to your company?" For the right buyer, all or most of the seller's $8 million in contributions would go to the bottom line. Even if the buyer figures it would need $6 million in overhead to handle the seller's revenues, that still leaves $2 million that would fall to the bottom line.

Should You Get an Appraisal for Your Lab?

Business appraisers are people who offer the service of valuing a business. In my humble opinion, business appraisals aren't helpful. They merely put a valuation number in the seller's head, and that number quite often doesn't make any sense because the appraiser's valuation techniques are mostly guesswork. Sure, the guesswork can have impressive methodology. I'll be generous and call it an academic exercise.

The only true measure of a company's worth (what someone else will pay for it) is missing from academic exercises. Beyond providing a number rooted in no rational basis, the appraisal may raise the seller's expectations and cause the seller to reject the market value of the company. Worse, the actual market value of a company may be perfectly suitable to fund the seller's desired lifestyle, but that high appraisal number may lead the seller to opt against selling the business.

What do buyers think of an appraiser's valuation? They don't. The valuation of an independent appraiser, someone with no skin in the game other than the fee he's charging the seller, is of zero value to the buyer. A business appraisal isn't worth the paper it's written on.

Bottom line: Sellers should let the market decide the value of their businesses.

The Asset Sale vs. the Stock Sale

There are many considerations when selling your business, and among them are determining whether to structure the sale as an asset or a stock sale.

One overlooked area of M&A is the question of what exactly the seller is selling and the buyer is buying. Companies themselves aren't really sold, per se; instead, the buyer is acquiring either certain assets of the company (in an asset deal) or the company's stock (in a stock deal).

Buyers typically prefer asset deals over stock deals because they are a lot cleaner. The assets involved may or may not constitute the entire company and often include intangibles, such as the company name, domain names, customer lists, work in progress, and sales pipelines. Asset deals are cleaner because the buyer is picking and choosing what to buy. The buyer picks the good assets and leaves behind the bad assets and some, or perhaps all, of the liabilities.

Here are a few reasons why buyers prefer asset sales:

- **Undisclosed liabilities are not assumed.** With an asset sale, only specific assets identified in the purchase agreement are acquired. This means that undisclosed and unknown liabilities are not acquired or assumed. If the seller has any undisclosed liabilities, such as potential lawsuits against the company, the buyer is well protected since those liabilities stay with the seller.

  In a stock sale, the seller would be liable for undisclosed liabilities that originated before the sale. Every stock purchase agreement will contain language to that effect. The process is different because a lawsuit for something that happened before the acquisition will probably name the new company, which the buyer now owns. The buyer then can use the purchase agreement to sue the seller.

- **NEWCO structure can be flexible.** If a buyer purchases stock, the buyer is stuck with the structure of the original company. In an asset sale, the buyer sets up a new company of his or her choosing (usually referred to as NEWCO during a transaction for the simple reason that the company usually isn't given a formal name until later).

  Some buyers prefer structuring the NEWCO as an LLC, because of the flexibility. For example, one big difference between an S Corp and an LLC is that an LLC can be set up so that profit flows per the operating agreement independent of ownership percentages. In an S Corp, the profit flows to the corporate owners by stock ownership percentages.

- **Asset sales boost cash flow by re-depreciating assets.** It is typical for a buyer to want to do an asset purchase that allows him or her to pay fair market value for the hard assets, then depreciate them. This hurts the seller because the government doesn't allow assets to be depreciated multiple times. The IRS charges the seller normal income tax rates (vs. capital gains rates) on the gain of the assets, as compared to the depreciated or book value. This is called depreciation recapture.

Why Structure as a Stock Sale?

As noted, most buyers prefer an asset sale, both to avoid undisclosed liabilities and for tax and cash flow reasons. Therefore, the majority of our acquisitions are structured as asset sales. There are a few reasons why a stock sale would be structured. The two most common are these:

1. There are a few large customer contracts that you don't want to change. With a stock sale, the contracts continue with no change. However, it is important to review the contracts and language specific to the change of ownership clause.

   In an asset sale, the contracts need to be changed or assigned to the new company that purchased the operating assets. It can be difficult to get certain contracts assigned in a reasonable amount of time and sometimes not at all (for example, large government contracts or "grandfathered in" state insurance contracts).

2. If the company being acquired is a C Corporation, then a stock sale avoids the double taxation issue of an asset sale. With a C Corporation acquisition structured as an asset sale, the proceeds from the sale of the assets flow into the C Corp. Corporate taxes are paid, but the net proceeds are still stuck in the C Corp. To get them out, the owners have to take wages or dividends and, thus, pay taxes again. It is a painful way to sell a business.

Regardless of the structure chosen by both the buyer and seller, there will be a thorough reps and warrants section in either agreement to help mitigate concerns of both the buyer and the seller. I will discuss reps and warrants in more detail in a later chapter.

Key Takeaways

» The value of a business is almost always dependent on earnings. It is adjusted earnings, called adjusted EBITDA, that are used for the valuation.

» Valuation comes down to how much money the business will produce in the future and the risk factors associated with generating that money.

» Less Risk = Premium Multiple.

» The average price paid for a business is five to six times adjusted EBITDA.

» The seven attributes that define a quality business and, therefore, are more likely to receive a higher multiple include clean financials, a solid management team, diversified client mix, compliance, solid future earnings, strategic locations, insurance contracts, and all of the above combined.

» Asset sales are preferred by buyers due to tax and liability concerns. A stock sale is necessary when certain contracts would warrant transferability. If the seller is structured as a C Corp, then a stock purchase would avoid the double taxation associated with an asset purchase and, thus, benefit the seller.

» Though it is not ideal, there are creative ways to sell a company that is operating at a loss.

» Skip business appraisals.

6

STEP 4
Market the Business

Once you have decided to sell your business, chosen your dream team of advisors, prepared your business to be sold, determined the potential valuation and best structure, it is time to develop the marketing plan.

The M&A advisor will assist your team in creating a competitive marketing plan. This chapter focuses on step four of the M&A process: marketing the business.

Marketing = Competitive Bidding = Maximum Selling Price

The sale of a business benefits from competition among buyers, as is the case with anything bought or sold. When a bidding situation develops, the selling price almost always goes higher, or the terms improve. Given that, it is interesting to look at how businesses are typically marketed and sold.

Small Businesses (Sales of Less Than $5 Million)

Small businesses are usually sold by business brokers. A business broker typically handles a dozen listings at once and doesn't have the time to do much, if any, custom marketing. Their marketing efforts are usually limited to running ads on the business-for-sale websites.

These ads are relatively simple. Selling a small business is like selling a standard automobile. A clinical laboratory that services physician offices is easily understood, so you would want to describe the location, size, and financial performance and include some photos. These ads typically appear on sites such as businessnation.com, dealstream.com, contractlaboratory.com, and businessesforsale.com.

This method is effective since small business buyers know to search these sites. Marketing on the websites makes sense for many small businesses, since these sites are geared to individual buyers who make up the majority of small business buyers.

Middle-Market Businesses (Sales of $5 Million to $200 Million)

A middle-market company needs an in-depth confidential business review that describes all aspects of the company, including target market, competition, history, service lines, number of patient service centers, and three years of financials.

The market for midsized businesses gets larger as the company gets bigger. Some individuals can still buy, but more often other competitive companies and private equity groups will be your target market. They can come from anywhere in the country or internationally. The key to getting the most attractive bids for middle-market businesses is to market the company to a large number of individual buyers, potential corporate suitors, and private equity groups, both domestic and international.

The key is to integrate industry networking and marketing techniques. Middle-market businesses are usually sold by M&A firms. This helps to ensure that you receive the greatest number of offers and attract the highest price.

Again, our team at Advanced Strategic Partners has spent our entire career in the laboratory industry. We have relationships established with the CEOs, CFOs, COOs, and boards of directors at most of the larger laboratories and private equity groups (PEGs).

Large Businesses (Greater Than $200 Million)

Large companies are like a Rolls Royce Dawn. There is a limited number of qualified buyers who will be interested, so you would hire a specialized broker who knows the laboratory industry and can approach the buyers within their network. A large marketing campaign is not needed. For large businesses, an investment banker or an M&A firm is typically hired.

Again, the advantage of hiring a firm like Advanced Strategic Partners is that each of our executives has worked in various positions within the laboratory industry. We know most of the key buyers and have the expertise to best position your laboratory to ensure that you receive the maximum value.

Marketing to Strategic Buyers vs. Financial Buyers

Strategic Buyers

A strategic buyer is an entity that is involved in the seller's industry who can enjoy synergistic benefits from the purchase beyond the face value of the stand-alone earnings stream, such as

- Attaining economies of scale,
- Reducing competition,
- Exploiting new technologies,
- Increasing buying power,
- Expanding geographically,
- Filling a weakness in the product or service lines,

- Providing enhanced opportunities for the employees,
- Establishing strategic alliances, and
- Eliminating redundant functions.

It is important to remember that, in the end, any acquisition needs to increase earnings for a strategic buyer. The value is always related to earnings. Strategic buyers don't pay a premium automatically. They'll try hard to buy at the lowest possible price, like financial buyers. It's typically a competitive bidding war that causes them to increase the bid. The difference is that they know they can increase the bid because of the extra value derived from synergies.

When selling a business, it is best to assume that there are no stupid buyers. Occasionally, we'll get a business owner who wants to put his business on the market for substantially more than it is worth. He hopes that a strategic buyer will see the unique qualities of his business and pay handsomely for it.

The strategic corporate buyers that we work with are not naïve. The best transactions in business sales are win-win, with everything disclosed, and at a fair price that allows the buyer to operate and enjoy the business. Though we typically represent the sellers, we make sure to structure a win-win that is fair for both parties.

Financial Buyers and Private Equity Groups

Financial buyers, typically private equity groups or wealthy individuals, are buying strictly on the financial strengths of the stand-alone company. They are simply trying to buy low and sell high, usually with a time frame of three to seven years. Financial buyers, as you can imagine, are adept at analyzing the financials, gross margin data, market data, competition, and other aspects of the deal. A strategic buyer will know many of those details since they are in the industry.

- **Typical middle-market PE committed fund.** A committed or dedicated equity fund is one where the investors have invested capital into the fund. A pledge fund is where investors have pledged to invest if the fund manager finds a suitable investment. A search fund or dry fund is where fund managers go out looking for opportunities, then come back to investors, often larger private equity, to obtain the capital.

- **Typical lower middle-market PE search funds.** Private equity firms often set a minimum level of EBITDA at $1 million to $5 million.

We received an email from a business owner who had a letter of intent to sell a majority interest of his lab to a private equity group, but he was having second thoughts. We told him that we would do some research since we had not heard of this group. We went to their website, which was obviously new, and they did show several transactions. The equity group was made up of several individuals looking for smaller deals from $500,000 to $1 million in EBITDA.

They ended up being a search fund or dry fund, so they didn't have the money in hand. They were searching for labs and would obtain commitments for the funding after they located and negotiated an LOI with a company. Some of them work with larger private equity groups or wealthy investors, and some use family money.

The important point to realize is that they don't actually have the money, and it is possible that they never will. These search funds range from opportunistic sharks, purely acting as deal finders, to trusted industry experts who are as good as gold in terms of raising the funds. It is our job to point out the differences and, when meeting with private equity groups, ask some pointed questions. If you're working with an equity fund, pose the following questions:

- Who are your investors? Are they private individuals, friends and family, or larger PE funds?

- What is the process and under what conditions do you get the money? This should be explained in detail. Make sure to understand if they have to pitch this opportunity from the ground up to investors or if they have some latitude in finding certain types of deals.

- Do you plan to use any debt and, if so, under what conditions will this happen? Are you dependent on raising debt?

Also, be clear on the terms in the LOI. It is common for private equity groups to present an offer in terms of total value or cash payment and then mention that the seller would retain equity in the form of an equity buyback. An equity buyback uses some of that cash.

Remember, you usually want some added value besides their money. If they are industry veterans who can pull together a good board of directors, add key employees, and use their knowledge to grow the company, then you can both win. That is why it is important to talk to their references from past deals. This is also why it can be important to get an M&A advisor involved.

Let's look at the difference between private equity and venture capital in more detail. As previously mentioned, PE firms invest in profitable companies while VC funds invest in start-ups. The PE firm makes the acquisitions by loaning the company money or arranging the injection of debt into the company, while a VC fund buys equity in the start-up.

A PE firm wants its portfolio company to continue to grow, so it may add other synergistic acquisitions, and then sell the company to another firm within a few years. Although enormous growth rates are desirable, most PE firms are realistic. They aren't seeking exponential growth, but rather good, solid geometric growth.

A VC fund is betting that the start-up will rapidly bloom into an enormous company (eBay, Microsoft, Uber, Google, and Apple are all examples of venture-funded start-ups). The VC fund expects its investments to experience exponential growth.

We have found that strategic buyers pay more for companies than PEs or VCs for a few reasons. As the name implies, "strategic acquisition" is exactly that. The acquirer is buying a company that has an important strategic fit, so the acquirer may be willing to pay a premium to keep a valuable company out of the hands of a competitor. They're often not bound by the same limitations as PE firms.

The investors in PE firms agree to invest only if certain parameters are part of the deal; not paying too much for a portfolio company is often a part of the PE mandate. Strategic buyers have more freedom to spend what's necessary to get what they need. Strategic buyers may be willing to pay a higher price because their strategy is to buy and hold long term. They aren't seeking to earn a return on the investment; they're seeking to earn a return on the cash flow of the acquired company's operations.

For middle-market laboratories, we have found that you really can't predict who is available and ready to buy at a specific time. Our group will create a business plan that includes specific buyers to target based on the best strategic fit. Typical numbers of prospective buyers end up being roughly five to twelve private equity groups and five to ten strategic buyers.

The marketing is always done in a blind manner so that prospective buyers don't know the identity of the company until they have signed a confidentiality agreement. Granted, sometimes it can be a challenge to craft marketing materials that don't give away the identity.

We have a thorough database that we have compiled with twenty-six years of industry contacts. In addition, we have a marketing specialist on our team who gathers strategic names from business intelligence databases, industry and trade journals, web searches, and, of course, our clients. There are always some short-list names that our clients don't want us to speak to based on previous interactions or discussions.

The following is an example of a marketing campaign that we recently implemented for one of our sellers. We took this laboratory to the market in August and closed in October of that same year.

- **June**—Prepared and gathered all corporate documents and completed a detailed fourteen-page confidential business review or "the book."

- **July**—Prepared the marketing plan, including the list of targets, and reviewed the details with our client.

- **August**—Launched the marketing plan with direct emails, mail, and personal phone calls to the thirty targets. There were twenty-eight interested parties who were required to sign confidentiality agreements.

  Sent twenty-eight prospects a copy of the confidential business review. Gathered six first-round offers out of the twenty-eight prospects. Conducted all on-site meetings and gathered four LOIs within a thirty-day established window.

- **September**—Finalized the LOI with the one chosen buyer.

- **October**—Conducted due diligence during a strict thirty-day allowed time frame.

  Signed and closed on all agreements, including the asset purchase agreement, noncompete agreements, transition services agreement, and employment contracts.

Ten Key Factors to Ensure a Successful Marketing Launch

1. **Fully prepare the company's marketing materials and financials before the marketing launch.**
   In addition to the confidential business review and financial analysis, we have produced short videos using a professional videographer. This allows the buyers to hear from the owner and to see the operations. The important point is that all materials should be prepared prior to the launch.

2. **Control the process.**
   A competitive process requires structure. You can't let the buyers dictate what the next steps are. It takes some discipline because strong buyers will have their own idea about what to do next. It is easy to get excited and potentially lose control of the process.

3. **Timing is critical.**
   We have a proven process that works in terms of launching a new company to the market. For example, if you email your strongest buyer prospects right away, they will likely respond right away. In addition, they will not need much time to digest the opportunity because they probably already know the industry and may be familiar with the company.

If you want to get other buyers involved, you will need to stall the stronger buyers that you contacted while others get up to speed. It is rarely a good idea to stall a buyer. If you look at the speed of the marketing channel (email, direct mail, calling, and print advertising vs. web advertising) and who the target is, you can proceed accordingly.

4. **Maintain momentum.**

Good timing means slowing things down just a little, so all buyers can reach the finish line (bids) at the same time. Good momentum means keeping the process moving and taking advantage of the enthusiasm of the buyers. Unfortunately, some buyers get left behind. A few large corporations can barely have their legal department turn around a confidentiality agreement in the time it takes for us to go through the entire bidding process.

We try to be patient and allow everyone time to catch up. We will attempt to get them up to speed later in the process, but some drop out. We would much rather keep the process moving and take advantage of the momentum than to stop and wait for one buyer.

5. **Publish dates.**

We publish dates for our selling process. The first date after launch is when questions are due. The second date is for the publication of the Q&A document and a financial update. The third date is when first-round bids are due.

The Q&A process, in which we publish all questions and answers to all buyers, is powerful in that it helps to create better informed buyers. It also ensures that all buyers know that there is competition (for example, a prospective buyer may receive fifty-five Q&As after having submitted just five questions of their own).

6. **Keep focused on business performance.**

   It is worth repeating that a common deal killer is a lack of performance during the negotiations. We have structured our process so that the owners can remain focused on their business. We typically have so many prospective buyers that having management conference calls with each one could stall the sale. The questions can get monotonous because each buyer generally asks the same questions: Why are you selling? How long will you stay for a transition? This is another reason our process includes a written Q&A document that allows the owner to answer common questions once.

   It is human nature for the seller to be distracted with the selling process: How many companies have responded? What do they think of my company? However, it is critical to stay focused enough to achieve the performance numbers that were communicated to the buyers. The deal depends on it.

   At Advanced Strategic Partners, we provide weekly written updates in summary form, so our sellers know where we are in the process and what potential buyers are saying about their company. In addition, we schedule one thirty- to sixty-minute call weekly to review this information with our sellers.

7. **Let the market dictate price.**

   The free market will tell you what the price is. We've had sellers who would have asked for much less than they got, a difference of millions of dollars. Although to be fair, we have companies that don't sell for what the owners had hoped to get. With an exhaustive effort to market the company to a broad market, at least we know it was a price determined by a market of multiple buyers.

8. Control the meetings.

Instead of having a buyer meeting occasionally throughout the process, which can be quite disruptive, we go through a "first-round bid" process where each interested buyer must submit a nonbinding indication of interest that includes price, or at least a price range, and an indication of the deal structure. We then present an analysis of the first-round bids to the client and decide together whom to meet with. Therefore, the client meets with qualified buyers who have already indicated what they would pay. In addition, the meetings are scheduled within a relatively short amount of time, sometimes in sequential days.

A common mistake is to accept invitations to buyer meetings as they come up early in the process. The business owner will spend significant time and energy with buyers who end up offering low bids.

9. Have options.

We would like to think of our job as providing options to our clients. Often, a client will say that private equity doesn't make sense, so why waste the time? There may be some private equity firms that own similar medical companies where a strategic fit exists. From our experience, you don't know where the ultimate buyer may come from. In addition, each buyer will have a different price and idea about how to structure the deal. We execute a sales and marketing campaign with each engagement, bringing buyers along and presenting many options to our clients.

10. Keep everything confidential throughout the process.

Maintaining confidentiality is crucial for keeping the business healthy while going through the long sales process. The announcement of a pending sale can spook employees, customers, and suppliers. Most business intermediaries are well-trained in how to sell and market a business while preserving confidentiality. Occasionally, stuff happens, but we have witnessed dozens of businesses changing hands with few problems in this area. All it takes is a good business intermediary who follows an established process and stays aware of problem areas where leaks can occur.

How Do You Market a Company and Keep the Process Confidential?

For small or large businesses, the key is to create a campaign with a description that is enticing but doesn't include enough information to identify the company. To hide a company's identity, sometimes we'll make the location fuzzy (for example, "Southern-based" instead of Florida). We may include a specific project name instead of identifying the name of the actual laboratory. We work with the business to make sure that the owners are comfortable with the level of confidentiality of the blind marketing materials before we send them out.

Moreover, maintaining confidentiality is not difficult when dealing with professional investors and other companies as buyers, because they know the ground rules. Breaches can occur, but they are rare.

Should You Tell Your Employees?

We did some work with a specialty laboratory years ago that hired a competing brokerage company to sell the business. The employees were not supposed to know that the company was being sold. The company's CEO had loose lips, however, and eventually told most of his direct employees. The irony was that this CEO had no ownership in the company and ended up being a huge liability for the owner. Over the course of that next year, they were not able to secure any written offers. What happened during the year? All of the employees who knew that the company was selling put their resumes on the street to find another job. They did not feel like the company could be trusted and knew that, if it sold, they would most likely not have a position with a new owner. Fear, uncertainty, and doubt spread throughout the company. Many of the employees said it was a big relief after the company couldn't find a strategic buyer.

I know that not all of the employees were anxious, but it is natural for your staff to have concerns. It isn't uncommon for some jobs to be cut in an acquisition, whether because of redundant departments, such as billing and human resources, or because it's a good excuse to trim back.

Another issue is that you don't really know if a deal will close until it is closed. Every business intermediary who has been around has experienced this fact firsthand. There are many reasons a deal might not close, such as financials not being properly presented or contracts that aren't assignable. Therefore, disclosing a sale to employees can cause unnecessary anguish and damage the company if word gets out to customers or competitors.

Key Takeaways

- Marketing = Competitive Bidding = Maximum Sales Price.
- Fully prepare all documents prior to the marketing launch.
- Maintain the momentum during the marketing phase.
- Make sure that you have many options.
- Ensure confidentiality by incorporating and enforcing confidentiality agreements. Don't tell your employees.
- Ensure that the M&A advisor markets to strategic buyers, private equity groups, private investors, and venture capitalists.
- Publish dates and stick to timeframes.
- Control the meetings.

7

STEP 5

The Letter of Intent and the Due Diligence Process

You have made the decision to sell, created your perfect dream team of advisors, determined the likely value and deal structure, marketed the business successfully, and are at the stage of the letter of intent (LOI) and due diligence. What can you expect during this stage of the process?

This chapter focuses on step five of the M&A process and explains the letter of intent and due diligence in more detail.

Timing is important when planning to negotiate with buyers. You don't want to lose the individual momentum of any one specific buyer by starting too early and slowing it down because you need to allow enough time for other buyers to get up to speed.

We don't begin negotiations until after the buyers have submitted their first round of bids. Once this occurs, we like to ensure that the buyers have had a chance to visit and meet with the owners and management.

We conduct buyer and seller management meetings that further validate the confidential business review, video, and all conversations that we've had up to that point. For the sake of timing, we'll try to push all of the meetings into a fairly short time period. It is easier on our client to do them all at once rather than to spread them out over months. Our goal is to conduct this part of the process within less than thirty days for all potential buyers.

This is where negotiations start. The buyers have had ample chance to get their questions answered before first-round bids and have met with our clients to hear the story and see the company. This is the time that your M&A advisor will start the competitive nature of the process.

The Letter of Intent Explained

A letter of intent (LOI) outlines the terms of a deal and serves as the "agreement to agree" between two parties.

The LOI is nonbinding except for a few terms. The most notable of these include

- The agreement between parties that they will keep everything confidential (nondisclosure clause) and

- The agreement by the seller to break off talks with all other parties (no-shop or stand-still clause) for a period of time to allow the buyer to conduct due diligence, typically sixty to ninety days.

The majority of the LOI is nonbinding, and either party can back out for any reason. It is uncommon for that to happen because, at this point, both the buyer and seller have spent significant time and money leading up to the LOI.

The LOI defines what a deal may look like and allows the buyer some time to perform the due diligence to verify the information that has been presented. It is used as a roadmap for the attorneys when they craft the final purchase agreement and other closing documents.

It is important for the LOI to have enough detail so there isn't a lot of negotiating left on major deal terms. There is always going to be some negotiating, but you don't want to have to deal with something so major that it impacts the overall value of a deal.

The following items should be included in the LOI:

- Price and legal structure (asset or a stock sale).

- If there is an earnout (future performance-based compensation), there should be details about how that is earned. If there is any confusion at all, examples should be included.

- If there is a seller note, the LOI should contain the terms of the note and what, if any, security is on the note. If it isn't a straight note, a payment schedule as an exhibit can be helpful.

- Unless the seller is going away immediately, there should be details for the seller's future compensation.

- The status of the accounts receivables, payables, cash, and other money issues, and any net working capital requirements should be clear (for example, will the seller maintain any cash or accounts receivables in the business?).

- Every LOI is different and is based on the concerns of both the buyer and seller. The laboratory industry and its buyers use fairly standard LOIs.

While due diligence is being performed, attorneys will take boilerplate purchase agreements and similar documents and modify them to include the terms in the LOI. A four- or five-page LOI can't possibly include all details of an acquisition or investment, so there are always points and issues to resolve. Usually, these are resolved quickly and amicably. Some items are a little more challenging to figure out, but at that point, both the buyer and seller are committed to a deal and are able to compromise on a solution.

After an LOI is signed, it is due diligence time, and sometimes things go wrong for various reasons. A competitive environment with multiple buyers is preferred because most of the time the losing bidders will stay in backup positions to buy the company. That provides a peace of mind for the seller during the due diligence process.

What Is Considered Appropriate Due Diligence?

Simply put, due diligence is an "open book" time. It's when the prospective buyer gets to investigate a potential acquisition to make sure that the business is in the condition represented by the seller.

Medium–Large Business Due Diligence

As mentioned previously, due diligence starts with a nonbinding letter of intent to purchase. A definitive purchase agreement is usually not created until after due diligence. We have, however, had aggressive closings when we facilitated the purchase agreement during the due diligence. Due diligence can range from a little more than a "book check" to a team of ten to fifteen attorneys spending months researching a company. Typically for the middle market, it consists of some sort of quality of earnings analysis by financial analysts as well as legal, compliance, and technical due diligence.

The following areas will be reviewed during the due diligence phase:

- Financial books and records
- Incorporation documents
- Employee benefits, policies, and compliance issues
- Internal systems and procedures
- Customer contracts
- Intellectual property
- Condition of assets
- Customer and vendor interviews (limited basis)
- Review of all business and legal contracts
- Any key areas of concern identified while negotiating the letter of intent

Fortunately, many of the items on the detailed due diligence list don't apply in most instances, so you can mark them "NA" for not applicable and shorten the ordeal to something more manageable.

Paper or Electronic Deal Room?

The majority of due diligence is done via electronic deal rooms. The cost of these services has come down substantially in the last few years. Firms like Firmex or V-rooms are built for due diligence and have audit trail capabilities that include features such as watermarking documents.

A more cost-effective service such as Dropbox or Google Docs is also adequate. We have clients who have their documents organized in hard copy format. This is not the ideal situation, but it can work.

In the instance of a paper-based system, the buyer will send a team to the seller's site to review and copy the needed documents. At Advanced Strategic Partners, we subscribe to an electronic deal room service and offer this service to our clients. In addition, we offer our clients the added service of assisting in the early preparation of gathering and uploading documents to ensure a successful due diligence.

Keep the Deal Moving

As previously mentioned, delay is the most frequent deal killer, and due diligence delays are among the worst. Normally, due diligence is sixty to ninety days, but some deals stay in due diligence for six to nine months. The entire process can be tough and take its toll on everyone. The owner must run his company and respond to continued requests for information. It is critical to have an assigned team of internal and external folks working on the due diligence process.

Should you disclose everything in due diligence? Your liability as a seller is far less if you disclose rather than hide, especially during the due diligence phase.

Sample: Shortened Due Diligence Request List

The following is a shortened due diligence request list used in many of our lab deals. For a more extensive list, schedule a face-to-face meeting with our firm once you have decided to sell your business. We would be happy to provide you with this detailed information.

Short Due Diligence List

1. **Organization**

- Copies of articles of incorporation, bylaws, and shareholder/ Board of Directors minutes or consents for the past three years for the company and its subsidiaries.

- Organization chart listing all legal entities which are part of the company or in which the company has any ownership interest, including ownership structures.

- Copies of all state certificates where the company is registered as a foreign corporation or other entity.

2. **Real Estate**

- Description of any real estate owned by the company and copies of related deeds, mortgages, surveys, title insurance policies, certificates of occupancy, easements, condemnation orders, and zoning variances.

- Schedule of all real property leased or used by the company, which includes the following information regarding the premises: address, square footage, monthly rent, use, end date, landlord name, and whether landlord is a physician, customer, or other.

- Copies of all real property leases; any amendments to such leases, and a diagram of the premises with dimensions, including both exclusive space and any common space within the suite (not common area elsewhere in the building).

3. **Personal Property**

- Copies of records (lists, computer printouts, descriptions, floor plans, process flows, etc.) relating to the description, value, location, maintenance, and condition of the machinery, equipment, and other personal property owned by the company.

- List of all leased equipment and other tangible property by department with lessor, age, amortization reserve and method, remaining lease terms, annual lease payments, and buyout price.

- Copies of leases for any personal property.

4. **Operations**

- List of all tests performed in-house, including billable CPT codes, with monthly volumes for the last two fiscal years and the current fiscal year to date along with the production schedule showing turnaround time.

- Provide the number of in-house tests and the number of reference tests, by month, for the last two fiscal years and the current fiscal year to date.

- Provide the total accessions, by month, for the last two fiscal years and the current fiscal year to date.

5. **Accounts Receivable**

- Fee schedules for all payer classes: client, patient, insurance, Medicare, Medicaid, including all CPT codes used.

- List of clients with specialty indicated and monthly revenues broken down by payer.

- Billings for each type of payer and customer and frequency of billing and payment terms.

6. **Personnel**

- Employee census showing name, title, current salary, or hourly rate with shift differential listed, date of employment, location, dependent status, whether exempt or nonexempt.

- Provide the number of full-time employees for the last three fiscal years and the current fiscal year to date, each by month, if available.

- Organization chart companywide and by department.

7. **Retirement Plans**

- All current, signed, and dated plan documents for any and all retirement plans (including both qualified and nonqualified defined contribution plans, defined benefit plans, and deferred compensation plans).

- In addition to all current plan documents, all plan amendments for each current plan.

- All Internal Revenue Service approval letters for all plans; these are called determination letters and/or advisory letters or opinion letters, as applicable. The different labels apply to the different types of approval letters depending on the plan.

8. **Welfare Plans (medical, dental, disability, flexible spending account)**

- All current, signed, and dated plan documents for all welfare plans, including any and all amendments.

- The signed and dated Forms 5500 for all welfare plans for the most recent three years, including any accompanying schedules, reports, and attachments.

- All insurance policies relating to the coverages provided under all welfare plans.

9. **Benefit Plans—Additional Items**

- All excerpts from the employee handbook discussing any benefits.

- A statement regarding whether any plans provide coverage to retirees or former employees.

- A statement regarding whether all contributions to all retirement and welfare plans that are accrued or will be owed based on employment up to the closing date have been timely made and are current. If contributions have not been made, a statement of the estimated amount owed.

10. **Financial and Accounting**

- Consolidated sales/gross profit statements for the past three years.

- List of top ten tests, with CPT codes, performed by dollar and volume for the past twelve months.

- List of top ten vendors by dollar volume and category of products purchased the past twelve months.

11. Taxes

- Copies of federal, state, and local tax returns for the last three years, including income, franchise, sales and use, property, payroll, and other taxes.

- Provide detail on any accounting book/tax book differences as of the most recent year end for the company.

- Information on pending or closed federal, state, and local audits, appeals, or private letter rulings.

12. Bank and Credit Arrangements

- Copy of all documents and agreements showing evidence of all outstanding borrowings of the company, whether secured or unsecured, including loans and credit agreements, indentures, promissory notes, bank lines of credit, and other evidences of indebtedness and all guarantees.

- Copy of guarantees or indemnity undertakings given by the company.

- Copy and description of amounts and other terms of any indebtedness between the company and any of its officers, directors, employees, consultants, physicians, or customers.

13. Insurance

- Copy of any broker agreement currently in effect.

- Listing of each business insurance policy currently in effect indicating type of coverage, carrier, policy number, policy dates, limits, deductible, claims made or occurrence and annual premiums.

- Liability claims experience (currently valued) by year for the last five years for each policy.

14. Information Technology

- Provide an inventory of all commercial and proprietary applications/systems in use, include copies of licensing.

- Provide listing of all hardware (for example, PCs, business system platforms), date acquired, last upgrade, date/cost of planned replacement or upgrade, estimated remaining life.

- Describe scalability limits and expansion needs assuming continued revenue growth.

15. Marketing

- Copies of any documents which describe compensation to the company's sales and marketing staff.

- Outline of sales department, staffing, management, territories, etc.

- Copies of all marketing materials currently in use.

16. Billing

- Provide all documents establishing the Medicare, Medicaid, RRMC, Tricare-Champus, Schips, and FEHBP programs (referred to as the "Federal Programs") that indicate the company is qualified to participate in those programs.

- Copy of confirmation from the enumerator (NPPES) of the company's NPI(s).

- Provide a copy of the form CP 575 or other official documentation from the Department of the Treasury–Internal Revenue Service, which shows the Employer Identification Number (EIN) assigned to the company.

17. Compliance

- Reports given to the Board of Directors and any documentation related to Board resolutions or actions related to compliance.

- Reports/logs of issues raised through the compliance program.

- Internal auditing activities, policies, procedures, and protocols.

18. Licensure and Certification

- Does this laboratory perform in-house developed tests? If so, provide a brief description of the method. For commercially distributed kits, indicate the FDA status of the kit.

- Copies of all health regulatory licenses, permits, certifications, and approvals pertaining to the company issued by governmental agencies ("Permits") including CLIA certification, state licensure, FDA approval, CAP accreditation.

- Descriptions of all enforcement actions or threatened enforcement actions initiated by any governmental agency or any correspondence or notice received from any governmental agency or private person with respect to compliance of the company's operations.

19. HIPAA

- Copies of all HIPAA Privacy & Security policies and procedures.

- Description of any contact received from the OCR regarding HIPAA complaints.

- Copy of HIPAA privacy complaint log.

20. Environmental Matters

- Copy of any internal company reports concerning environmental matters relating to current properties or properties formerly owned or operated by company.

- Description and copies of all notices of violation, complaints, suits, or similar documents by the Federal Environmental Protection Agency or any state department of environmental regulation or any similar state or local regulatory body, authority, or agency.

- Copy of medical waste transportation, storage, and disposal policies and procedures.

21. Litigation

- A schedule of all legal claims, suits, actions, arbitrations, administrative proceedings or governmental investigations, pending or threatened, providing a brief description of (a) parties, (b) nature of the proceeding or investigation, (c) date commences.

- Any consent decree, supervisory agreement, settlement agreement, or other agreement entered with any governmental agency or third party (including any entered within the last three years which may have lapsed or terminated or which are pending).

- Letters that have been sent to the company's accountants by lawyers and other third parties in connection with the company's audits completed in the last five years.

22. Prior Business Acquisitions

- List of all business acquisition transactions during the prior five years, whether by stock purchase, asset purchase, merger, or otherwise.

- With respect to each business acquisition transaction, (a) copies of all related agreements (with schedules and exhibits), (b) closing documents, (c) preclosing due diligence reports and analyses, and (d) documents related to post-closing purchase price.

- Provide a list of any and all vendor and or employee director related disputes in direct correspondence with the business acquisitions.

Key Takeaways

- » The LOI outlines the terms of a deal between the two parties. The majority of items are nonbinding.
- » Have your M&A advisor assist in the preparation and organization of the needed documents for due diligence prior to taking your company to the market.
- » Create an electronic deal room to properly organize all documents during the sales process.

8

STEP 6

The Definitive Purchase Agreement, Tax Structure, Earnouts, and the Close

Once you have made the decision to sell, hired your dream team of advisors, determined the likely valuation and structure, prepared your marketing plan, signed the LOI, and completed due diligence, it will be time to finalize the purchase agreement and accompanying agreements.

This chapter focuses on step six of the M&A process and takes a closer look at the definitive purchase agreement, tax structure, earnouts, and the close.

The Definitive Purchase Agreement

The purchase agreement is a final binding agreement between the buyer and seller. This agreement is either a stock purchase agreement (SPA) or an asset purchase agreement (APA). The purchase agreement is usually initiated by the buyer. The documents are lengthy and detailed. The key point to keep in perspective is ensuring that the document accurately represents the major facets of the deal. Most purchase agreements contain legal jargon that doesn't differ from one agreement to the next.

The purchase agreement can be from forty to one hundred pages long. This book would be far too long if I covered every item in a purchase agreement. Some of the main items are these:

- Legal names and addresses of the buyer and seller
- Specifics of a stock or asset sale
- Defining what is being purchased and what is excluded
- Intents of the buyer and seller
- Terms of the purchase price, including cash, stock, notes, earnouts, and escrow amounts
- The anticipated closing date, actions, and deliverables
- Reps and warrants of the sellers and buyers
- Covenants and agreements, including employee matters, transfers of warranties, prorations, accounts receivable, and accounts payable
- Indemnifications, including those of the sellers and buyers, survival of the reps and warrants, adjustments to the purchase price, and manner of payment
- General provisions, including expenses, severability, waivers, public announcements, jurisdictions, and interpretations
- Exhibits and schedules

Deliverables will accompany the purchase agreement, such as these:

- The company's articles of incorporation and bylaws

- Specific documents for all accompanying exhibits, including leases, personnel, payroll, financials, client lists, test volumes, reagent and equipment lists, and payer contracts

- Stock certificates providing evidence of ownership

- Stock books, ledgers, corporate records, seals, and minutes

- Closing financial statements

- Signatures from both parties for the escrow, confidentiality, noncompete, nonsolicit, and employment agreements

In addition to the main business items and exhibits, there will be a complete reps and warrants section. Reps and warrants are essentially promises that the seller and buyer make. Most agreements use standard boilerplate language from agreements previously completed.

It is expected that sellers should expect to make reps and warrants on past known events but not on future events that are unknown to the sellers.

It is common to provide the buyer with reps and warrants specific to everything provided throughout the due diligence and sales process. It is best to ensure that you use terms recommended by your legal counsel, including "to the best of seller's knowledge." We have seen purchase agreements with twenty to thirty pages specific to the reps and warrants section. These should be taken seriously.

We have seen several of these areas addressed in the reps and warrants section:

- Seller is the owner of the shares or assets and free from liens.

- Seller has the legal right to sell his or her shares.

- The company has full corporate power and legal rights to deliver the agreement.
- The company is in good standing.
- The sale of the company doesn't violate or conflict with any rules, regulations, or government authority.
- The company has filed all required tax returns.
- Seller has made all corporate documents available to buyer.
- Change of control will not trigger some sort of material change, such as an agreement with a major customer that allows the customer to cancel a major contract.
- No options, warrants, or other agreements pertaining to a claim of the company's ownership are outstanding.
- Seller has provided a complete list of all contracts and agreements between the company and other parties to the buyer.
- Seller owns the property and all assets being sold.
- Seller has paid all taxes.
- Seller has provided the buyer with all material contracts, mortgages, leases, employment agreements, severance agreements, employee benefits, vendor and supplier agreements, reagent and equipment agreements, PSC agreements, and much more to be itemized.

- Seller has supplied all patents, patent applications, trademarks, trade names, service marks, customer lists, and copyrights to the buyer.

- All computers and computer software, including any proprietary databases owned or licensed by the company, are paid for or owned by the company and properly disclosed to the buyer.

- Seller has provided a complete list of all accounts payable and accounts receivable.

- All inventory that has been presented is accurate and usable.

- All financial statements, including cash flow, income statements, and balance sheets, have been accurately reflected.

While you are completing the definitive purchase agreement, exhibits and documents, it is important to think through your tax strategy. We have included a brief overview of several items for consideration. Please consult your accountant for professional advice.

Tax Structures

As previously mentioned, C Corporations are a challenge to sell. Buyers usually prefer to buy the business assets out of the C Corporation, leaving the seller with two levels of taxes, one at the corporation level on the sale and the other when the owner takes the sale proceeds out of the corporation as wages or dividends. In this instance, it is better for the seller to sell the entire corporation (that is, sell the stock). Buyers usually push to buy assets, but often a stock sale is better for the seller.

It's surprising how many business owners make the important decision to sell and only later figure out how much they will have to pay in taxes and fees. It is far better to figure it out ahead of time so that you have an idea of how much cash you'll end up with in a transaction. If you happen to be a C Corp, have your tax consultant figure out the net proceeds of the sale for both a stock sale and an asset sale. Once this is done, you will understand the difference in tax cost. The best way to handle the sale of a C Corp is to let the buyer know up front that you are selling a C Corp and that it must be a stock sale.

Ordinary Income vs. Capital Gains

Much of your effort when selling your business is to move as much value into capital gains and pay capital gains tax, not ordinary income tax.

Long-term Capital Gains

The favorable capital gains tax is based on the gain in the value of assets purchased then sold after holding the assets for at least a year. Technically, it's the long-term capital gains tax rate, but in business sales, practically everything is held longer than a year, so it's often just referred to as the capital gains rate.

Goodwill

Goodwill, which is an asset, is defined as the difference between the purchase price and the price of the hard assets. Goodwill is taxed as capital gains and can be written off by the new owner through amortization over a period of fifteen years.

Ordinary Income

Ordinary income is taxed at a higher rate. The ideal goal is to minimize components of a deal that are taxed at ordinary income tax rates. You can't get completely away from paying the higher tax rate, but you want to avoid it as much as possible. For example, business buyers will want a noncompete agreement, and there will normally be some value assigned to it. Any value assigned to noncompete agreements and consulting agreements are taxed at the ordinary income rate.

Depreciation Recapture

This one is a surprise for many business owners. The IRS allows you to depreciate and write off assets at a certain rate that helps effectively lower your tax burden. If you later sell those assets for more than what you wrote down, the IRS will expect you to pay back the tax savings.

For example, say you depreciated some equipment down to $2,000 (book value) but then sold it for $5,000 (fair market value). The government essentially says, "We gave you the tax benefit of writing it down to $2,000, but it turns out that it is worth more than that, so pay us back." The depreciation recapture amount of $3,000 is taxed as ordinary income.

Wages

Wages are at the bottom in terms of compensation for selling a company. If a buyer offers the seller a sweet consulting package for five years without the seller actually having to show up for work, it really isn't so sweet. Why? Not only does the seller pay ordinary income taxes on it, but he or she also gets hit for Social Security payments.

Asset vs. Stock Sale

An asset sale, for tax purposes, means that a deal is structured so that the buyer acquires the underlying company assets instead of purchasing the entire corporation (the stock).

In an asset sale, the buyer acquires a specific set of assets, including inventory, equipment, goodwill, accounts receivables, and payables. Each asset has a distinct tax attribute. Therefore, you would calculate your taxes on how the purchase price is allocated between these assets. The allocation is a negotiation point between the buyer and seller. The hard assets transferred are stepped up to the purchase price, and the buyer gets to depreciate the new basis.

In a stock sale, the entire corporation is transferred unless specifically excluded in the purchase agreement to the buyer, including the company name, bank accounts, and contracts. The depreciation schedule is transferred, allowing the buyer to continue with the same schedule.

In general, the IRS sets up a conflict between a buyer and a seller, which can cause protracted negotiations on the allocation of the purchase price. Payments that get favorable tax treatments for a seller will usually create a negative tax effect for the buyer. For instance, goodwill is taxed at the capital gains rate for the seller (good) and depreciated by the buyer instead of expensing that cost immediately (bad). The consulting contract mentioned earlier would get taxed as ordinary income to the seller (bad), but the buyer gets to expense those charges right away (good).

Deferring Taxes

You can defer taxes on the sale of a business in a few ways. Except for a seller note or an earnout, most of our clients don't take advantage of these.

Seller Notes

Seller notes normally qualify as installment sales with the IRS, so taxes are not due until you receive payment. Many sellers do not wish to take a note for a portion of their business.

Earnouts

An earnout (performance-based payout) may also be taxed when you receive payment.

Tax-free Mergers

If you take stock in a company for a substantial part of the consideration, you won't pay taxes on the gain until you sell that stock. These arrangements should be called tax-deferred mergers instead of tax-free mergers. There are a lot of rules and regulations regarding tax-free mergers and when stock can be sold. It is best to get tax advice early in the process.

Structured Sales

There are ways to use an insurance company to set up an annuity, which is only taxable when you receive the money. To use structured sales, you must set the process up well before the transaction. A key to the tax deferral is that you cannot receive money from the transaction because then the IRS essentially says, "You've got the money now, so you pay the taxes now." The monies have to go directly to the life insurance company. The good news is that you get to specify a payment schedule, and it can be just about anything you want. The bad news is that you can't change the payment schedule once it starts.

Charitable Remainder Trust

Another popular tax deferral method is a charitable remainder trust (CRT). This one is especially attractive if you have a charity you would like to support. A CRT is an irrevocable lifetime trust that will pay you at a rate based on current interest rates. The trust must be set up to designate a 10 percent payment to your charity of choice when you die. The investment vehicles that you can use within the trust are flexible. There are a variety of schedules for the payout, including a fixed percentage of account balances.

In addition to understanding the tax consequences, I wanted to spend some time discussing earnouts.

Earnouts

An earnout is a contingent future payment based on specific performance milestones. For example, in a simple earnout arrangement, an extra payment of $100,000 to the seller may be "earned" by growing the company by an additional $1 million in revenue in the first twelve months after the close of the transaction. Earnouts are sometimes used when there is a difference of opinion on what the earnings will be in the future. The buyer says, essentially, "Show me." They are also used to protect against risks like high customer concentration.

Some of our clients tell me that they would never accept an earnout. They believe that the historical earnings don't tell the whole story. In other words, the seller wants the buyer to pay more for a high future earnings probability.

Unfortunately, many buyers don't want to pay more money for revenue that isn't a guarantee. That is when earnout discussions begin. Here is how to tell if an earnout makes sense when you sell your business:

Businesses Are Bought for Future Earnings

In looking at earnouts, it is useful to remember that what a buyer really cares about is future earnings. Since we don't know what future earnings will be, we generally use historical earnings for valuation. Earnout discussions naturally arise when there is a significant difference between historical earnings and future projections.

Let's look at a few scenarios of historical versus projected earnings.

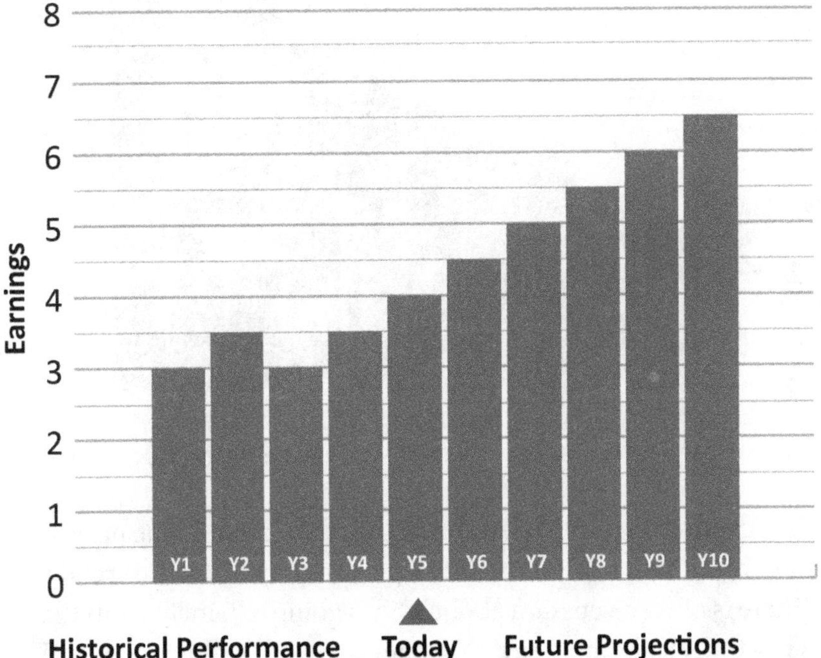

Scenario 1—Stable Earnings. This company has a stable history and believable future projections based on a track record of performance. In other words, the risk is fairly low, and the seller should not expect an earnout.

The purchase price in this case should be composed of cash and possibly a note. Unless there are other risks, the note shouldn't be contingent on revenue or earnings, and there should generally not be an earnout.

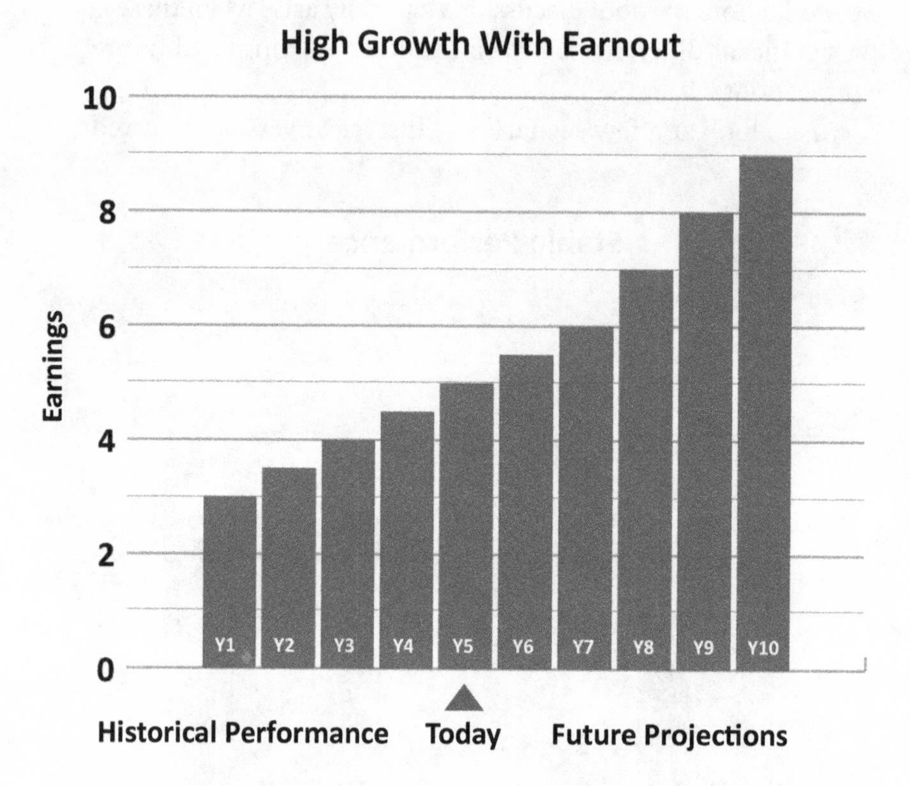

Scenario 2—Supported Growth. In this scenario, the projection of future growth is clearly supported by historical trends. There is often discussion about who is going to benefit from the growth. A seller may say, "You can see what will happen, so I want to base the purchase price on a higher multiple or possibly use next year's earnings."

A buyer may say that if the company grows, it will be because of his or her efforts after they purchase the company, not because of anything that the seller has done. After all, they certainly aren't buying it to give all of the earnings to the previous owner.

A smart seller will counter this by explaining that much of the future growth is because of the foundation they have built. For example, the website, reputation, product, recently signed contracts, services, and other components have all come together to build momentum.

What the seller is also saying is, "Trust me on this." No one likes to bet millions trusting someone whom they recently met, so this is typically where earnout discussions start.

In this type of scenario, an earnout could look like this: A base price of cash and notes is calculated using historical performance, and an earnout is structured based on whether the company achieves certain targets. The target may be revenue or an earnings milestone.

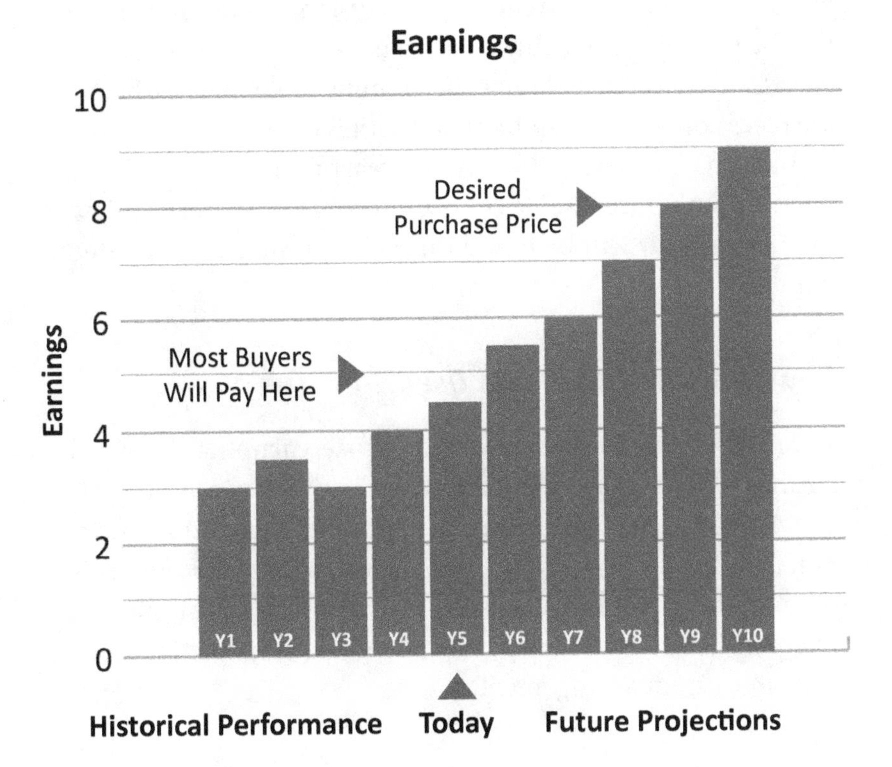

Scenario 3—Unsupported Growth. Occasionally, we see a scenario where the company doesn't have an obvious upward trend, yet the business owner believes that there are many growth opportunities. The owner may say, "We opened two new patient service centers last month and expect sales to take off." Charting this situation looks like the Unsupported Growth chart.

In this case, the buyer has a good case to say, "Well, if I spend the money and time to invest in sales and marketing for these two new patient service centers, I will be able to enjoy the rewards." Sometimes we can negotiate an earnout in this type of scenario, but it depends on the situation and why the seller believes growth is inevitable.

Scenario 4—Recession-Proofing a Transaction. Although earnout agreements are mostly seen in growth companies, we've also seen them used a few times to protect the buyer. For example, the economy may be entering a recession, or the government may be imposing price cuts on certain testing. Many companies have seen a retraction of sales and earnings from the time before the recession and during pricing declines.

In scenarios where the buyer is fearful of future declines, they will set a purchase price on a lower base number. Achieving the earnout will be based on maintaining these targeted numbers.

How Often Are Earnouts Used?

Small businesses generally don't use earnouts. In small business transactions, there are typically short transition periods. Sellers "earn" an earnout by staying during a transition. Financials can be messy, so measuring earnout milestones is problematic. Buyers want to come in and operate the business as theirs without any of the operating limitations that often occur with an earnout arrangement.

An earnout is fairly common for larger companies in the lower and middle markets. Valuation gaps between buyers and sellers are common, which can lead to discussions on earnouts.

Structuring an earnout can be a challenge. Typical issues that need to be worked out include determining

- How to measure the earnout,
- How long to make the earnout period, and
- What operational limitations will be placed on the buyer.

Earnout Period

The earnout period should be between eighteen months and two years. If it's too short, the seller has an incentive to act in a short-term manner. If the earnout period is too long, it can delay the integration with the buying company.

The length of the earnout depends on how long the seller remains involved in the business. Naturally, the seller wants some control of the company during the earnout period to ensure that the company achieves the targets.

Amounts in Earnouts

It is hard to provide much guidance on the amount since it depends on the deal and how much earnings risk the buyer is trying to mitigate. We have seen earnouts ranging from 5 to 30 percent of the purchase price, although 20 percent is the most common.

A buyer will prefer to base an earnout on EBITDA. A seller's most common fear is that he will not have control over costs and, therefore, cannot control EBITDA. An experienced deal attorney told us that earnouts cause the most lawsuits after a deal is closed. For this reason, we try to negotiate earnouts based on revenue milestones, not EBITDA. If we fail at that, gross margins can work. The further up the profit and loss statement you go, the easier it is to measure an earnout.

You can also measure earnouts on events such as signing, or often re-signing, a major contract, launching a new testing line that was in the pipeline prior to selling, and other milestones.

Keep in mind that complex formulas based on revenue, gross margins, or earnings are problematic when it comes to writing the language into a purchase agreement. It's easy to brainstorm and draw creative graphs and curves. It is best to create a simple formula that can be easily explained in a legal agreement.

Controls and Restrictions

A seller will need to place a few controls and restrictions into the earnout agreement. These are some of the restrictions or buyer covenants that are put into place during the earnout period:

- Offices will stay in the same locations.
- Key employee(s) will not be terminated.
- Sales compensation structure will remain the same.
- A certain amount of capital will be invested into a project.

Each restriction is a negotiation point. The key is to structure everything as simply as possible. For example, it is easy to say that a key employee cannot be terminated, but what if he or she steals from the company? You can stipulate that sales compensation will remain the same, but maybe the new company uses a different healthcare package. You could argue that this changes the compensation.

These issues need to be covered in the definitive purchase agreement. The issues that need to get worked out in earnouts tend to run much deeper than anticipated. It isn't uncommon for earnouts to disappear late in negotiations when the parties determine that there are too many issues to address.

The Close

Once you have successfully finalized the definitive purchase agreement, noncompete agreement, and an entire array of requested check-off items provided by attorneys on both sides, it is time for the closing. The closing is rather mundane and is as simple as exchanging signed documents and waiting for the monies to show up in your bank account.

Key Takeaways

» Take the time to understand the differences between a stock purchase agreement (SPA) and an asset purchase agreement (ASP). Review the reps and warrants sections with your attorney and understand their significance.

» Address key tax issues and implications in the beginning of the M&A process.

» Determine if an earnout makes sense in your situation.

» Understand all components of the earnout and keep things simple.

A sample purchase agreement and noncompete agreement from our team can be obtained by emailing and scheduling a face-to-face meeting. I look forward to discussing the possibility of working together once you have decided to sell your company. These documents will be made available to those companies who sign an exclusive listing agreement with our firm, Advanced Strategic Partners.

m18butterworth@advancedstrategicpartners.com

9

89 Key Takeaways
to Maximize Your Laboratory's Value

1. **Coordinate Your Exit Strategy.**
   Before selling your business, it is imperative that you meet with your advisor a minimum of six months before the sale. This will provide everyone with a better understanding of the lab transaction process and the necessary preparation. We recommend that you upload all of the needed due diligence documents to a cloud-based system prior to taking the business to the market.

2. **An Increased EBITDA = An Increased Selling Price.**
   This is the single most important factor when it comes to increasing value, unless you are considering an asset-only sale. An asset-only sale may be a great alternative solution for some sellers, especially if the EBITDA isn't attractive as a stand-alone operation. Our team will assist in the initial review of your financials and make recommendations. In each situation, we will apply the buyer's metrics to determine an adjusted EBITDA.

3. **Understand the Critical Role That Revenue Cycle Management Plays in Your Laboratory.**
   Put in the proper processes and tools to effectively manage the entire revenue cycle in your laboratory. This includes

monitoring the front and back end of the revenue process to include patient encounters, coding, documentation, claims management, compliance, financial reporting, patient billing, and collections.

4. **Increase Laboratory Profitability by Implementing a Comprehensive Revenue Cycle Management System.**
   Through the reduction in claim denials and processing errors on the front end, this will increase the lab's profitability.

5. **Understand Your Laboratory's Contractual Allowances and Current Contracts.**
   Put in the proper automation to eliminate the human error of possibly accepting partial payment from claims where money has been left on the table.

6. **Understand the Revenue Recognition Guidelines.**
   Understand the Sarbanes-Oxley Act (SOX) and the most recent revenue recognition rules of the Financial Accounting Standards Codification (ASC) 606.

7. **Look for Ways to Reduce the Laboratory Operating Expenses through an Automated Revenue Cycle Management System.**
   This includes bad debt expense in addition to unnecessary overhead in the billing department.

8. **Diminish Working Capital Needs.**
   A midsized business is sold with enough working capital (current resources less present liabilities) to continue operating the business. Demonstrate that you can diminish this sum now, and you can take more money home from the transaction later.

9. **Become an S Corp vs. C Corp.**
   In the event that you determine it will be several years before you sell your business, check whether you can take an S Corp status. Most buyers will want to complete an asset deal, and the twofold tax assessment made by a C Corp can kill a transaction for the seller.

10. **Broaden Your Client Base.**
    It is important to have a solid mix of Medicare, client bill, and third-party payer business. In addition, it is equally important to have a broad range and number of clients. They should produce a sustainable price per accession and industry standard number of tests per accession. Having one physician client or hospital client with 15 percent or greater of your business isn't attractive to a buyer.

11. **Make Yourself Irrelevant.**
    What business would you rather purchase? The one where the owner is never available because he or she is always traveling or the one where the owner needs to come in because the place will fall apart without him? A business that depends intensely on the proprietor gets far less money.

12. **Pay Uncle Sam.**
    Realistically, everyone wants to avoid paying taxes. There are a lot of personal expenses that get run through businesses. Your advisor will review your financials and determine an adjusted EBITDA so that your business looks more attractive to buyers. The expenses should be explained to buyers during the sales process. It is far more intelligent to pay your taxes for a couple of years before a deal is completed to avoid any future issues with the transaction.

13. **Understand the Term Adjusted Earnings.**
    Before you take your company to the open market, work with your advisor to determine an adjusted EBITDA. For instance, a few costs will be legitimate modifications, so there would be no compelling reason to chip away at those costs, while different areas may require some genuine cost-cutting and improvement.

14. **Make Your Business Desirable.**
    Do you have any legalities holding you back? Are there any anticipated monies owed? Buyers despise risk, and that can bring down the cost of a transaction deal. Recognize and fix these issues prior to entering a deal.

15. **Hire a Financial Planner.**
    A financial planner can disclose what you should net from a transaction to achieve your monetary objectives. Many laboratory owners think it is premature to hire one before they cash out. We urge our sellers to start talking to one early on.

16. **Get a Legal Checkup.**
    If you have a lawyer, request that he or she ensures that all legal documents are up-to-date. You should designate an internal person to monitor and organize employee contracts, licenses, personnel issues, regulatory and compliance, lawsuits, and other legal documents.

17. **Be Prepared for a Six- to Twelve-Month Sales Process.**
    The transaction process doesn't depend on the size of a company. It takes about six months to complete a transaction if everything goes right. Realistically, though, nine to twelve months is the most common time frame.

18. Organize All Corporate-related Documents.
You will be requested to deliver all documents that confirm your business's financial standing (three to five years minimum), salary and personnel information, income and accounting reports, leases, insurance contracts, policies and procedures, equipment and reagent costs, board of trustees' notes, licenses, and so on. An experienced representative can help you with this process.

For a detailed list of the 450+ items that most buyers request, please contact us and schedule an appointment to discuss the possibility of using Advanced Strategic Partners to represent you during the M&A process.
We look forward to hearing from you at:
m18butterworth@advancedstrategicpartners.com

19. Get All Accounting and Financial Statements in Order.
Meet with your CFO, bookkeeper, controller, and accountant to ensure that the financials are together and that your taxes are filed and up-to-date. This includes income statements, cash flow statements, balance sheets, and the general ledger of the company. Most midmarket businesses are sold with reviewed (not audited) financial statements for the three years prior to a transaction. On the off chance that you are considering selling in the next couple of years, get your financial statements in order.

20. **Be Mentally Prepared a Year to Eighteen Months Prior to the Sale.**
    A year or two preceding a sale is an ideal opportunity to begin getting mentally prepared. During this time frame, it will be imperative to concentrate on controlling expenses and boosting income.

21. **Have Realistic Expectations about Your Company's Value.**
    Get a realistic number of what your business is worth. The market will dictate the value during the sales process. Your M&A advisor will be able to share his or her experience with recent transactions.

22. **Make Sure Your Business Looks Good in Person and Behind Closed Doors.**
    Ensure that your sites look impeccable at all times. This will make your business more appealing to a buyer. Though it is important to look good on paper, you should have all of your laboratory sites, patient service centers, and other venues in order.

23. **Create a Dream Team of Advisors.**
    You will need a transaction M&A advisor, M&A healthcare lawyer, CPA, and a financial advisor to assist with the sales process. In addition, you should designate a small internal group of trusted senior-level employees to assist in the information gathering that will be required during the due diligence phase. We recommend having your CFO or controller, COO, VP of HR, or VP of compliance. Also, make sure that everyone signs confidentiality agreements early in the M&A process.

24. **Hire an M&A Advisor from the Laboratory Industry.**
    We recommend using a broker or M&A advisor for

companies with earnings larger than $1 million. The key is to locate someone who understands the lab industry and who has a track record for closing lab transactions.

For more information on Advanced Strategic Partners and how we can assist you, email us at:

m18butterworth@advancedstrategicpartners.com

25. **Locate an M&A Healthcare Attorney.**
    Get yourself the best legal representative in the healthcare industry. On the off chance that your lawyer doesn't have experience with business deal exchanges specific to the healthcare industry, hire one who does. Your M&A advisor will know the best attorneys based on their history of working on prior deals.

26. **Call References.**
    Request and call references from prospective intermediaries, attorneys, CPAs, and financial advisors.

27. **Ask about Any Potential Up-front Fees.**
    Most M&A businesses charge up-front fees. That fee should be utilized to showcase the business, not to pay substantial commissions to the sales representatives or M&A advisors.

28. **Don't Allow Delays during the Sales Process.**
    Delays kill deals. Make sure to get your financials, contracts, leases, and the confidential business review prepared before starting the sales process with prospective buyers. It can cause a dent in the deal if a buyer requests this information and you don't have it readily available.

29. Go beyond the Internet for Marketing.

The universe of business buyers is much bigger than the websites that display the businesses that are for sale. To get the most value, you have to contact and connect with serious buyers. Our firm has relationships with the majority of the key laboratory C level executives, private equity groups, and venture capital groups.

30. Pay Attention to Private Equity.

The field of private equity is developing and is notwithstanding redirecting capital from people in general markets. The healthcare industry remains at the forefront of their attention. Your advisor should have access and knowledge of the probable candidates.

31. It Is a Global Marketplace.

Make sure that your M&A advisor is someone who thinks out of the box. Ambry Genetics made headlines in 2017 with their sale to Tokyo-based Konica Minolta for $1 billion.

32. Send Buyers to Your M&A Advisor.

Buyers will regularly get in touch with you directly because they may not know that you have hired an advisor. Your advisor can spare you a great deal of time qualifying these buyers and walking them through the transaction process. Make sure to send all buyers directly to your M&A advisor.

33. Find More Buyers.

It is unlikely you will locate a buyer who will be willing to pay full price for your business. An advisor can assist you in finding more buyers and to ensure that you can have a backup plan in case the deal falls apart with the first buyer.

34. **Be Honest and Forthcoming.**
    Uncover negative data at an early stage. It is much better and less problematic than unveiling it later. Keep in mind that there is no perfect business. They all have negative data.

35. **Don't Give It All Away.**
    You don't have to reveal everything immediately. Your M&A advisor will know when to present what key information during various phases of the sales process (for example, key clientele, insurance contracts, competitive strategies, and insider facts should all be revealed during the due diligence phase).

36. **Always Have a Confidentiality Agreement in Place.**
    Have confidentiality agreements signed with your advisors, prospective buyers, and your key trusted internal senior staff. Everyone who is involved in the M&A process needs to have a CA in place.

37. **Ask Specific Questions of Buyers.**
    Know who you are doing business with. Are they a good match for you and your company? There may be a time when you will have to take a part of the sale in cash, stock, and possibly earnouts.

38. **Make Sure That There Is Always Growth.**
    There is nothing like a drop in sales or income to put a transaction on hold, potentially until the end of time. Being easily distracted during a transaction process can be a problem. Utilize an advisor to assist in leading the sales process while you stay focused on continuing to grow your business.

39. Don't Waste Your Time.

Don't spend too much time in meetings and discussions with prospective buyers. Let your M&A advisor coordinate questions and answers through a detailed written process between your advisor and the prospective buyers. Once you have received all of the letters of intent, it will be time to become more involved as an owner.

40. Do Employees Need to Know?

Most buyers prefer not to cause undue worry over something that may take numerous months to complete or may not occur at all. On the off chance that employees find out about a possible sale, it is best to tell them that you are investigating alternatives for strategic partnerships. It is never a good idea to let them know that you are in the process of selling the company.

41. Talk to Your Senior-Level Employees.

Make sure that any senior-level employee who is involved in the M&A process signs a nondisclosure agreement and confidentiality agreement. Keep the team small and manageable. You will want to offer incentive bonuses to ensure the success of the process.

42. Remember Your Employees.

There is a good probability that some of your employees assisted along the way in getting your business where it is today. It would be smart for you to consider a bonus at the end of the deal so that they will feel appreciated. This will ensure that the transition goes smoothly for the new buyer, clients, and the employees.

43. Be Consistent.

Buyers, being normally mindful about the measure of cash that they could be spending, will ask similar inquiries again and again, searching for irregularities. Make sure that your advisor coordinates and leads all meetings throughout the process to keep track of the project.

44. **Talk the Talk and Walk the Walk.**
If you are expecting enormous growth and want to be paid for it, share the risk with the buyer. This can be structured in an earnout during the contracting phase.

45. **Prepare for the Emotional Roller Coaster.**
The lab transaction process will likely take you on an emotional roller coaster with many highs, lows, twists, and turns. This is typical and expected during this kind of process.

46. **Don't Get Personal.**
One of the key reasons to hire an M&A advisor is to keep the buyer and seller from becoming too involved with each other during the deal. It is best to let your M&A advisor deal with the buyer on a day-to-day basis to avoid any conflict between the two.

47. **What Is Your Buyer's Agenda?**
Understand the buyer's objectives to determine how you can assist in achieving the overall goals. Often sellers get carried away thinking that they are the ones who should be courted throughout the process. It is important to understand the needs of both parties to ensure a win-win.

48. **Show Them the Money.**
A strategic buyer will be reviewing the previous three to five years of your business's financials to determine an adjusted EBITDA. This adjusted EBITDA will be based on numerous factors, including the
    - Potential combined synergies of the laboratories,
    - Personnel,

- Combined synergies of the patient service centers, and
- Contractual allowances.

It is important to show the buyer that you understand what the potential is and to demonstrate what the revenue, expenses, and earnings could be.

49. Do You Really Have a Serious Buyer?

A few buyers may get irritated that they have to share their account information and capacity to buy before being provided with any confidential data about a business. These buyers are no good. A good M&A advisor can weed through these types of so-called buyers. Your advisor should have experience working with the buyers on previous deals and will know who the real players are.

50. Do You Know Enough about Your Buyer?

Make sure that you do your research on your buyer. Review all prior laboratory transactions. Again, your M&A advisor will know how to weed out those buyers who aren't serious.

51. Not So Fast.

Buyers may request on-site meetings to see the seller's business. There is no need to do this until they have provided your advisor with an idea of what they would be willing to pay.

52. Visit Their Website.

If you are talking to a private equity group (PEG), then it is important to visit their website to see what companies they have worked with in the past. Ask for references to determine if they have a track record of investing in the laboratory industry. Our team at Advanced Strategic Partners has built relationships with most of the laboratory active PEGs, which enables our sellers to avoid wasting unnecessary time.

53. **Show Me the Money (again).**
Numerous groups concentrating on the lower midmarket are called search funds or dry funds. They discover businesses, sign LOIs, and go to financial specialists afterward for the capital. Inquire as to whether they can really issue a check or access cash. It is important to understand who the end buyer is. Again, this is something that Advanced Strategic Partners is familiar with and will help with throughout the transaction process.

54. **What Is the Debt Structure?**
PEGs often utilize imaginative financing structures. It is important to ask how the financing will work on the proposed transaction.

55. **Understanding the Letter of Intent (LOI).**
Ensure that the LOI is specific. This incorporates the amount that a potential buyer will pay in cash, earnouts, stock, and other arrangements. Nonetheless, recall that the vast majority of the data on the LOI is nonauthoritative. Don't get hung up on it during LOI discussions.

56. **Ask Again.**
PEGs sometimes speak a different lingo and both the buyer and M&A advisor may not always grasp what they are talking about.

57. **Can a Seller Gain a Second Nibble of the Deal? It's Possible, but "Beware."**
Rollover value or buyback of offers in the NEWCO can be a great way to get a second nibble of the transaction. For

example, a business we sold a while ago had the EBITDA increase by 40 percent during the last year. The ex-seller possesses 20 percent of the new business and is en route to match what he walked away with during the first transaction. We have seen this go in the opposite direction where sellers have taken a portion of their deal in stock and ended up regretting it because of the loss in value, not to mention the loss of being able to control the outcome due to the new ownership control.

58. **Competition Is Key.**
    The most effective approach to get the best price for your business is to let the market drive the cost up. We pride ourselves in being able to create competition during the process due to our experience and successful track record. This is the primary reason you need to hire an M&A advisor.

59. **Price and Terms.**
    Most deals have many moving parts, and it can be a challenge to keep them in context. It is imperative to take the time to understand every one of the terms that will characterize your transaction. Get your legal counsel involved once you have negotiated the price and business terms. Don't allow the attorneys to take control of the business issues.

60. **Cash Isn't Always King.**
    Though cash almost always gets the deal, be advised that the deals that offer the most cash up front aren't always the best deals. Review all aspects of the deal, including the structure, tax consequences, future earnout potentials, and stock options.

61. Earnouts Aren't Always Best.

We have seen a number of deals with an overdependence on earnouts. If you have a demonstrated, stable business and sensible expectations of value, there is no compelling reason to negotiate an earnout. There are numerous moving parts of an earnout, and as a previous owner, you will never again control most of those moving parts. Be careful before you get hung up on earnouts.

62. Earnouts Can Be a Possibility.

If you have a developing business or have recently signed several new contracts that will increase your revenues substantially, you may want to consider the possibility of an earnout. Work with your advisor to structure something that can be managed objectively.

63. Take Your Time.

There is a big difference between rushing the process and ensuring that you stick to deadlines. Keeping things moving is imperative; however, there is no compelling reason to rush the process. For example, we have seen the due diligence phase extended on several of our deals past the LOI deadline. This is normal due to various issues that arise during the process. It is important to compromise in certain areas while being strong in others.

64. Drive the Process.

Your M&A advisor should drive the process. This enables sellers to maintain the stability of their businesses.

65. Speak Up During the LOI Phase.

Once you have received the LOIs and have had a chance to review them, make a list of areas that should be addressed. If you have any concerns, you should address them. In any case, as I have said previously, a considerable number of items on the LOI are nonbinding.

66. **Bound or Unbound LOI.**
    Most terms of an LOI are nonbinding. There are some terms, such as the no-shop/stop and privacy that are binding. Talk to your legal counsel and M&A advisor and understand the difference.

67. **Noncompete Agreement.**
    You will be required and should be prepared to sign a noncompete agreement. The buyer has a privilege to run the business for a while without stressing over whether you will destroy it once you leave. In the event that you are contemplating competing in a related field, wait until due diligence is done and have your lawyer bring it up. Doing it early may scare the buyer off. Your attorney will advise you on the average length of time required based on your state's laws.

68. **Work on Working Capital.**
    A buyer will require working capital, generally stock and accounts receivable less payables, to maintain the business. When all is said and done, for bigger transaction deals utilizing EBITDA, you should show that the business has enough working capital to maintain itself. For small businesses, it is debatable, and the seller usually keeps and gathers their accounts receivable. Make inquiries and know where you are on this issue.

69. **Understand the Tax Implications of C Corps.**
    Understand your company's existing structure and the tax consequences of a transaction. These issues should be investigated with your CPA sooner rather than later.

70. Should You Do a Stock or Asset Sale?
It is important that you understand the difference between a stock and an asset sale. The issue is fundamentally about expenses, tax consequences, and progressing risk. Make sure to address these issues with your counsel, CPA, and lawyer so that you're fully versed.

71. Buyers Prefer Asset Sales.
Buyers usually go for, and often demand, asset deals since they lower taxes, improve income, and place past obscure liabilities solidly on the seller.

72. Detailed LOIs Are Okay.
The more you can get worked out on the LOI, the smoother the due diligence and documentation stage will go.

73. Cloud-based Is the Way to Go During Due Diligence.
The cost has decreased significantly for the data cloud systems that have watermarks, review trails, and other conveniences (such companies as Firmex, V-rooms, and Deal Interactive). If you are innovative, you can utilize the complimentary data record sharing clouds like Dropbox or box.net to share due diligence documents.

74. Your Attorney Works for You.
It is important that you proactively give your attorneys clear direction. We recommend that you incentivize them to get the deal completed by establishing clear objectives, deliverables, and expected completion dates. This should include a backend bonus for completing the deal on schedule.

75. Put Your M&A Advisor to Work.
It isn't over until it's over. Utilize your advisor to determine issues that surface and to keep the momentum going.

76. **Assign Someone Internally to Manage the Due Diligence.**
    In a perfect world, you will have a representative (frequently a controller or office supervisor) who has been assigned to assist in the preparation of selling your business. This individual can deal with the everyday handling of the ongoing, unlimited requests for documentation.

77. **Stay Focused.**
    While you are experiencing the due diligence process, the buyer will watch your execution. Ensure that the business is still growing.

78. **Look for Proprietary Test Offerings and/or Relationships with Vendors.**
    If the company has proprietary test offerings and/or vendor relationships, this can become a highlighted selling point.

79. **Size Makes a Difference in Valuation.**
    Most buyers prefer to purchase larger companies. The average size of the laboratories that tend to gain more value are those in excess of $20 million.

80. **Profitability Matters.**
    The only asset more attractive than a profitable company is a highly profitable and growing company.

81. **A CA Agreement Typically Addresses These Sections.**
    - Use of materials
    - Disclosure of materials
    - Who's covered
    - Destruction of materials
    - Chain of command
    - Period of enforcement and jurisdiction

82. The Confidential Business Review, the Deal Book, and/ or the Information Package.

The main sales document in the mergers and acquisition process is the confidential business review. The most common name is "the book." The seller's advisors write this document. The information needed to write this document is typically provided by the owner's CFO. A well-written document takes forty-five to sixty days to write and becomes the document that allows a seller to obtain offers for his or her business.

83. There Is a Critical Document That Is Often Overlooked during the M&A Process, Called the Transition Services Agreement (TSA).

The transition services agreement is the key document that talks about a list of services that will be a part of the transition plan post-sale. Your organization will need an experienced laboratory M&A advisor to walk you through the negotiations of this document.

84. What to Do at Closing.

Get all signatures on the dotted line.

85. What to Do After the Closing.

Enjoy the victory and take some time to enjoy the important things in life. Also, make sure that the transition to the new buyer is seamless and smooth. This will ensure that everyone wins in the end.

86. Revisit Your Financial Planner.

All right, we know the reality. You never got a financial planner prior to this transaction. In any case, now it is truly time to hire one. Gaining large sums of money has a considerable number of traps that one can fall into. Your financial planner can assist in keeping you out of trouble.

87. Fulfill Your Obligations.

If you agreed to a transition period in your deal, give 100 percent to make it a success. It is the right thing to do. If you agreed to an earnout, assisting the business in its continued success will pay off.

88. Remember the Six Key Steps to Ensure a Successful Exit.

- Prepare Your Laboratory to Be Sold
- Create the Perfect Dream Team of Advisors
- Determine the Value and Structure
- Market the Business
- The LOI and Due Diligence
- The Purchase Agreement, Tax Structure, Earnouts, and the Close

89. The End Game.

I spent a lot of time thinking about the title for this book. The reality of our business is that most of us started in the laboratory industry because we have a passion for patient care. At some point in time, we have all anxiously awaited the test results of our own blood evaluation or for someone we love. This is one of the hardest moments of our lives. I remember when my mother received the phone call from her doctor, confirming her diagnosis of multiple sclerosis in 2000. We may not get the results that we had hoped for. However, a proper diagnosis allows us to proactively move forward with treatment and solutions.

As the laboratory industry has continued to consolidate, and the government has continued with steep reimbursement cuts, this has forced many lab owners to sell, retire, and cash in on what started as a passion for patient care. As each one of you embarks upon what is most likely the most difficult decision of your life—to sell or not to sell—our team at Advanced Strategic Partners would like to assist you in maximizing your value.

If you ask our clients what they remember most from working with us, they will tell you that by working with our team, we made them far wealthier then they could have ever imagined. Several of the lab owners suggested, "Why don't you write a book to help other lab owners?" thus, *The End Game* evolved.

Acknowledgments

This book would not have been possible without the support and encouragement of my mother and number one mentor, Ellen Butterworth.

Ellen, who was born in Lynchburg, Virginia, is one of five siblings. My grandmother was a registered nurse, which was unusual for a woman during her era. My grandfather was a high school teacher and a farmer. They worked hard to raise my mother and her four siblings while providing everything that they possibly could. My mother was raised in a modest home and didn't have much in terms of material "stuff."

Ellen worked several jobs to pay for her own college education. As far back as I can remember, my mother was always hard-working and intuitive. She has a quality that few people possess, one that I consider to be the true reason behind her success. She is bright and genuinely cares about people. She has the ability to walk into a room, assess the situation, and take definitive action in a short period of time. Most importantly, she listens. She is by far the most extraordinary sales executive I have ever met. Her true love, like my grandfather, was in teaching.

She started her career as a mathematics teacher and quickly learned that there was no money in teaching. She left her passion of teaching and went into computer sales during the 1980s—during an era when the technology industry was booming. She was at the right place at the right time.

Mother rose to the top of the computer industry, working for Entre Computer Corporation and eventually Digital Equipment

Corporation. After climbing to the top of the industry as the worldwide Senior VP of one of the largest computer companies, she decided that management was overrated. She desired to go back into a direct sales contributor role where she could best utilize her skill set, make her own schedule, and better control her income stream.

On a Sunday afternoon back in the 1990s, my mother found an advertisement in the local Atlanta newspaper from a company that was searching for an experienced computer sales executive. Who would have ever thought that it would be that specific newspaper ad that would forever change my mother's and my family's ultimate destiny?

The person on the other end of that ad was a young man by the name of Michael Dell. They were searching for someone to open the Atlanta market and to assist in getting Dell computers into the larger corporations. Again, my mother was at the right place at the right time. She successfully launched a new market in the Southeast for Dell computers that had many of the top industry CEOs in need of computerization and technology.

My mother was one of several talented people who put Dell on the map. She became one of the many "Dellionaires" who were created from that incredible company. She was able to retire by the time she was forty-seven. It is hard to believe that she retired at the age that I am currently, as I write this book. It is even harder to imagine having to live with the diagnosis that my mother was given the same year she retired. After all, retirement is supposed to be the best time of a person's life. It's the perfect time to sit back, travel the world, and enjoy the fruits of your hard labor.

Truth be told, my mother hadn't felt well for most of her adult life. One would never have known because she always had such a great attitude and outlook on life. Looking back, we suspect that my mother had been living for more than twenty years with multiple sclerosis. This included having received several misdiagnoses after seeing several dozen doctors. Finally, she was properly diagnosed with MS in 2000, three weeks before my mother and I had our "double wedding" ceremony with our new husbands in Jacksonville, Florida.

Mom, you are my inspiration, mentor, and hero. I am proud to be the woman that I am today in large part because of you! You have raised the standards for what women across the world should strive to be. I am proud to be your daughter. You gave me the single greatest gift in the world. You have always believed in me and encouraged me to reach for the stars.

To Bohdan Lucky, my great stepfather, mentor, and business partner, thank you for all your support these last two decades, particularly over the last ten years. This has been an incredible and fulfilling journey in so many ways. You taught me to "suck it up" and press forward when I thought I couldn't move another inch. You have managed to fill in the gaps and missing pieces of my puzzle. I couldn't ask for a better stepfather and business partner.

I also thank my amazing and handsome father, Edward Butterworth, who is an incredible businessman, father, and friend. Your sacrifices along the way are greatly appreciated.

A remarkable cast of characters in my life have given me inspiration along this journey, and I thank them: Davian and Jessica, my friends and newest adopted family members; Dr. Gary Winfield, the most successful, intelligent, and accomplished friend that anyone could ever have; Jed and Paul, my brilliant and inspiring closest friends and world traveling buddies (Jed, only you know how hard this road has been for me, and your friendship and advice along the way will never be forgotten); Nicole and James; Gary; P Daddy; the three Michaels in my life; Jack; Stewart and Maggy; Beth and Stuart; Pat and Paige; Eric, the best fashion designer and stylist ever; Lucy and Ayla; Eddie; Leslie; Hatcher; Audrey; Bo; Christine; Hannah; Aleksa; Bebe; Lucky; Hector; Mily; Nim; Andy; Jorge, my photographer; Kadir, my change agent who pushed me to create a new image after twenty years; and my executive assistant Mely (God blessed me when He brought us together). I admire and appreciate each and every one of you and thank you for your unwavering support through this journey.

Also, to my editor Sandra Wendel, who took charge, told me the truth, and taught me more than anyone during the book writing process, including how to achieve my own "end game" by helping me cross the finish line.

In addition, I am grateful for my upbringing and the amazing business folks who have surrounded me since I was a young child, including my late uncle Ben Soyars (senior executive with Philip Morris) and my late grandfather Hatcher Connelly, who was an amazing longtime teacher, farmer, and physical fitness educator. Also, my grandmother Catherine Connelly, an RN, devoted wife, mother of five, grandmother of twelve, and great-grandmother to twenty-one. Last, but not least, thank you to my grandparents Julian Harris Butterworth and Elizabeth Moore Bishop Butterworth, whom I never had the chance to meet. Your sacrifices along the way haven't gone unrecognized.

I would also like to acknowledge several companies in the laboratory industry that have taken the road less traveled and that have created a lot of success along the way. Thank you for your support and encouragement during the time I was writing this book. I have included information about these organizations at the back of this book.

I wish you much success in all your endeavors as you continue making such positive impacts in our ever-changing laboratory industry.

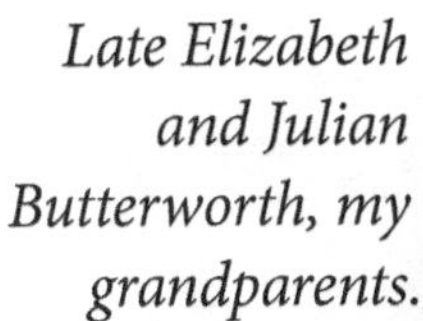

Late Elizabeth and Julian Butterworth, my grandparents.

Late Hatcher Connelly, my grandfather.

LONG-TIME EDUCATOR HONORED BY FAMILY, COMMUNITY

Late Ben Soyars (my uncle) and Little Johnny ("Call for Philip Morris").

Ellen Butterworth (my mom) with Michael Dell.

About the Author

Melissa Butterworth is an experienced mergers and acquisitions professional specializing in the laboratory industry. During the past twenty-six years, she has closed over $1.2 billion in deals specific to the clinical, molecular, and anatomical laboratory industry.

Along with her stepfather Bohdan Lucky, she founded Advanced Strategic Partners in Ponte Vedra Beach, Florida, in 2007. The company is a specialized M&A firm dedicated to providing laboratory industry expertise, market knowledge, and professional insight in structuring new revenue sales and marketing programs, business valuation, and M&A transaction advisory services. Clients range from hospital system and public laboratory companies to small to midsized laboratories.

Prior to launching Advanced Strategic Partners, Melissa spent fifteen years in laboratory sales and business development and held several key positions, including executive director of sales for a hospital outreach program, regional VP of sales, and national VP of managed care for a privately held Canada-based laboratory that went public in the US in 2000. She served as the director of hospitals for the Southeast division for one of the largest publicly traded laboratories in the US. In addition, Melissa has worked closely with a number of reputable national molecular testing companies.

In the course of her work, she advises laboratory business owners in the sale of their companies or the acquisition of other companies (seller and buyer transaction advisory services). She contacts the buyers and sellers, prepares businesses to be sold, negotiates and structures the deals, oversees the due diligence, works with the attorneys to draft the purchase agreements, and ensures that the majority of the deals that she is involved in cross the finish line.

Melissa's desire is that this book helps laboratory owners to become more educated about the M&A process and the necessary steps to implement, so they can maintain their original corporate integrity and mission for the community, patients, employees, and customers while maximizing the sale of their businesses. One of the most significant advantages of working with her company is her ability to provide new revenue sales and marketing program considerations to boost sales prior to selling.

For more information on services offered,
please visit our website:
www.AdvancedStrategicPartners.com

A special thanks to the
following organizations.

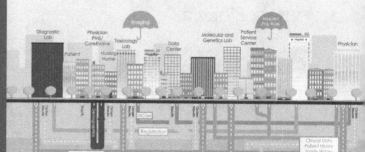

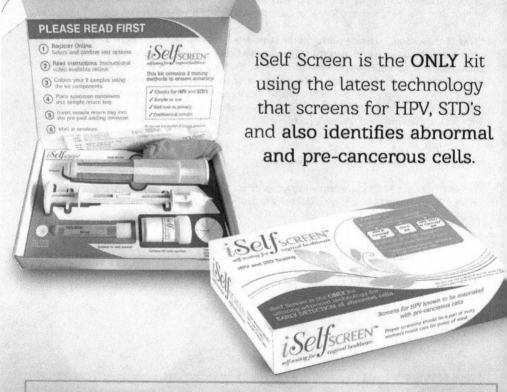

"Implementing strategies to improve business outcomes"

- Virtuosic Consulting, LLC has fifteen (15) years of clinical laboratory experience, as well as fifteen (15) years of healthcare financial experience
- The company has experience in all payment methodologies related to risk based and value based compensation, including ACOs and MACRA
- Collaborating with revenue cycle/billing staff to maximize your financials
- Long term relationships with payers and providers have proven to be beneficial in increasing revenue
- Developing payer strategy, market share analysis, and product evaluation
- Founding Board Member for non-profit foundations, organizations
- Develop bylaws, lead planning meetings, SWOT analysis
- The company understands the importance of integrating with your organization to accomplish goals through project management, strategic planning, business development and effective communication
- Virtuosic Consulting focuses on performance driven, measurable results to drive better business outcomes
- Virtuosic Consulting provides services to:
  - ✓ Non-profit foundations, organizations
  - ✓ Health systems
  - ✓ Hospice facilities, including palliative care physician groups
  - ✓ Independent physician groups
  - ✓ Employed physician groups
  - ✓ Independent laboratories
  - ✓ Commercial laboratories
  - ✓ Independent pathology groups
  - ✓ Employed pathology groups

E-mail: Virtuosic.Consulting@gmail.com

Linkedin: www.linkedin.com/Sarah Sallas-Herring

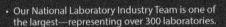

CPSIA information can be obtained
at www.ICGtesting.com
Printed in the USA
FSHW012246310321
79963FS

9 781732 955509